MW00760903

The Messiah and Me

How a Jewish Girl from New Jersey
Survived the Sixties and Found Faith
Where She Least Expected

Linda Sogolow

authorHOUSE®

AuthorHouse™
1663 Liberty Drive, Suite 200
Bloomington, IN 47403
www.authorhouse.com
Phone: 1-800-839-8640

This book is a work of non-fiction. Unless otherwise noted, the author
and the publisher make no explicit guarantees as to the accuracy of
the information contained in this book and in some cases, names
of people and places have been altered to protect their privacy.

First published by AuthorHouse 1/22/2008

ISBN: 978-1-4343-6337-4 (sc)

Library of Congress Control Number: 2008900536

Printed in the United States of America
Bloomington, Indiana

This book is printed on acid-free paper.

This book is dedicated to my parents
Betty and Jerome Fingerhut
With love.

So is the word that goes out from my mouth:
It will not return to me empty,
but it will accomplish what I desire
and achieve the purpose for which I sent it.
Isaiah 55:11

Contents

First Words

Every time I wished upon a star, I asked for the same thing: I wanted to meet God. I imagined God to be an amalgamation of my Grandpa Lew, my Grandfather Poppy, Abraham Lincoln, and Santa Claus. A serious but kindhearted Higher Power dressed in white cotton sheets and smelling of cigar smoke and mothballs.

In the event my wish was granted, I intended to start things off by asking God to give me all the things my parents wouldn't let me have, beginning with a carton of comic books, a sleep-over party, and a cocker spaniel puppy. I was also going to check into the possibility of being placed with a childless couple where I would finally get all the parental attention I craved instead of constantly competing with all my younger siblings. It wasn't that I didn't love my family; I just figured it was time for a change. Besides, was it really fair for my parents to have so many children when there were other people who didn't have any?

As a tête-à-tête with God was something that didn't happen every day, I was also hoping to take this opportunity to clear the air about a few things. I was pretty certain God had been monitoring my behavior from his throne in heaven and keeping track of all the times I kicked my sisters under the table, pulled their hair, or tricked them into doing my chores for me. I figured I had to be in some kind of trouble.

I wanted to defend myself. I wanted God to understand that even when my conduct was bad, deep in my heart I wanted to be good. I wanted the opportunity to explain that there were reasons I did the things I did and that if God had to share a bathroom with three younger sisters, he might have some anger problems, too. I was planning to apologize for all the times I had misbehaved and was willing to throw in those times when it wasn't even my fault. The main objective here was to clear the air and try to get on God's good side.

But most of all, I wanted to ask God all the things I was curious about and didn't understand. I wanted to know how fish breathed, why I always fell asleep when I tried counting to infinity, how come my family couldn't have a Christmas tree just because we were Jewish, and a million other things that nobody was ever able to explain to me.

As things turned out, I did get my opportunity to meet God, only it was many years later and under circumstances I never could have imagined. And that is what this book is all about.

Chapter 1:
Once Upon a Time in New Jersey

I was always asking the big questions. From the time I wore ankle socks and Buster Brown shoes, there were so many things I needed to know. How do the stars stay up in the sky? Where do babies come from? What happens when we die? It was one thing after another and the older I got the harder the questions. I was an outspoken little girl who was intensely curious about the important things in life. My mother used to lower her voice an octave and say, "Linda is deep."

I was born in New York City but the only memories I have of the two years I lived there are driven by glossy black and white photos in the family album. Following the birth of my sister Donna, my family moved to a New Jersey suburb that was populated by veterans of World War II and practically overrun by their bounty of baby booming children. This was a time that has since been memorialized in films like *Back to the Future* and *Pleasantville*. It was a time when uniformed gas station attendants would wash your windshield, check your oil, and top off your windshield wiper fluid every time they filled your tank. A time when it was not unusual for entire families to sit around the table at mealtime and when the preparation of hot food involved more than venting and nuking.

One of my earliest memories is of my father escorting me around the neighborhood on starry summer evenings, serenading me with the classics. "Gee, it's great, after being out late, walking my baby back home; arm and arm, over meadow and farm, walking my baby back home." Holding my hand, he would point out the constellations and, having been a Marine Corps pilot, he knew what he was talking about. Under the spell of my father's undivided attention, I was dazzled by the beauty of the stars and amazed to learn that the earth was just another mass hurtling through space on its designated orbit.

I never really doubted the existence of God. But a few years later, when I was taught "scientific" explanations for the origin of the universe, I started to have my doubts about the teachers. The notion that a random collision of atoms could result in something as complex as a DNA molecule seemed to require infinitely more faith than accepting the obvious: the world simply had to have been created by design. After all, even something as mundane as a chicken pot pie couldn't spring forth fully formed and of its own volition. I became increasingly convinced that there had to be a sentient intelligence behind the poetic grandeur of nature, the complexity of the solar system, and the miracle of humanity.

It seemed like my mother was always having babies. In the beginning, there were girls. From what I've been told, I took the arrival of Donna pretty hard; I still have a note from my late Grandma Rachel advising me to love my little sister and to please stop trying to push her down the stairs. A year later when Gail appeared, looking like a creature from another planet with her dimples and golden hair, I was past the terrible twos and already resigned to sharing. And a year after that, when curly-haired, twinkle-eyed Rayna showed up, I welcomed her into my world as further evidence of my exalted big sister status.

After the repeated trauma of having to share my parents' attention with one interloper after another, I slowly came to appreciate the benefits of sisterhood. There was always someone to play with, to fight with, to make up with, and then to play with again. I felt terribly bad for "only children" who, according to my mother, had "no one."

As soon as it was possible to do so, my mother began dressing my sisters and me in matching outfits. This was many years before psychologists discovered how damaging this practice was to little psyches and might result in children growing up to be murderesses...or even chorus girls. We narrowly averted these fates since my mother permitted some minor wardrobe variations. For instance, we were allowed to make individual color selections; while we might all be wearing white skirts, my blouse would be blue, Donna's would be pink, Gail would wear yellow, and Rayna would usually end up with green. Not coincidentally, these were also our designated toothbrush colors. But my mother's ideal was for her daughters to be dressed identically and we had absolutely no choice but to go along with it.

Our most memorable ensemble involved black patent leather Maryjanes, white ankle socks, and the famous watermelon dresses. The watermelon dress was a pink and white gingham creation, trimmed in rickrack, featuring capped sleeves and an attached pinafore. The pinafore was embroidered with three separate scenes. On the far right, was an intact watermelon slice; in the center was a watermelon slice with one significantly missing bite; and finally, on the left, rested a forlorn piece of watermelon rind next to a poignant handful of seeds. This was more than just an ordinary dress; this was a statement on the brevity of life, a visual representation of the existential dread of annihilation. Well, maybe not. In any case, my sisters and I adored these dresses and were firmly convinced that they represented the ultimate in fashion. But being forced to wear matching outfits was another matter entirely.

My mother used to have herself a grand old time going about her errands in the company of her four identically dressed little girls, our long hair pulled tightly back in pony-tails and adorned with coordinating satin ribbons. Whether we were shopping for groceries at the Grand Union, stocking up on school supplies at Newberry's Five and Ten, or sitting on swivel seats at B and G's soda fountain drinking coffee egg-creams, we were quite a sight.

Understandably, people would stare at us. And after they had gotten their fill of staring from a distance, they would frequently come over and make comments, not unlike those made while viewing animal exhibits in a zoo. "Look, Gladys, this one is blonde." "The one on the end is a little plump, don't you think?" And at that point, more often than not, our curious spectators would start up a conversation with my mother. It drove me completely nuts. Not so much because I minded the attention, but because I knew it was only a matter of time before they would ask The Question.

"Are they quadruplets?"

Invariably, inevitably, this seemed to be the burning question on everybody's mind. Quadruplets? Quadruplets! How on earth could we be quadruplets? What were these people thinking? I was at least two inches taller than Donna, who was at least two inches taller than Gail, who was at least two inches taller than Rayna. How could anybody in their right mind possibly think that we were all the same age? And more to the point, how could anybody possibly think that eight year old me was the same age as four year old Rayna? I was deeply and thoroughly insulted.

"Do we look like quadruplets?" I would ask in a haughty manner that was intended to be ironic but invariably came across as rude.

My mother, who has never been rude to anyone in her entire life, would seize this opportunity to embark upon an extended conversation with some poor soul none of us would ever see again. She would assume the theatrical voice she had developed during her stint as an off-Broadway actress and provide detailed biographies on each one of her brilliant,

7

beautiful daughters. It was not unusual for this monologue to extend to my mother's own childhood and her distinction as the first young woman from Albany, New York to have enlisted in the Marine Corps. It was not unusual for this monologue to include my mother's years of study at the Fagin School of Drama and the American Theatre Wing. Neither was it unusual for this monologue to continue for well over an hour.

If she was feeling particularly loquacious, my mother might even throw in her favorite Shakespearean soliloquy: "The quality of mercy is not strain'd, it droppeth as the gentle rain from heaven upon the place beneath: it is twice blest; it blesseth him that gives and him that takes…" It was truly amazing how my mother could engineer practically any conversation in such a way as to make this passage relevant. In the meantime, my sisters and I would be standing around getting increasingly restless and kicking each other in the shins.

There was never any shin kicking on Saturday mornings. That was when the Fingerhut girls would sit on the back porch of our post-war split-level home while our father read us stories from the Bible. To four wide-eyed little girls, this was exciting stuff. Adam and Eve getting taken in by that serpent in the Garden of Eden, the noisy fiasco that brought down the tower of Babel, Joseph taking the heat from his brothers because of that infernal coat. I think the story of Moses was probably my favorite: how he went from being a helpless baby floating downstream in a basket to leading an entire nation out from slavery. Even if you don't believe any of these stories are true, you have to admit they contain irresistible drama.

Back in those olden days, back before color TV, before diet Coke, before the Beatles, that was when I was first learning about God. It wasn't so much from the Bible stories, because I looked on those as fantasy and fiction. It was the love, attention, and protection of my father that provided me with the foundation to later understand what it means when the creator of the universe implores us to look upon him as "our Father who art in heaven." Although my family was far from perfect, we always knew we were cared for, valued, and loved. People who grow up without experiencing these basic concepts find it difficult to embark upon an intimate, personal relationship with God. But I'm getting ahead of myself.

Throughout my childhood, I wanted desperately to be discovered. My sister Gail had been discovered by a modeling agent one Sunday evening when our family was having dinner at the local Chinese restaurant. I think four identically dressed little girls eating their chop suey and chicken chow mein with chopsticks was probably what caught her eye. But golden-haired, deeply dimpled, sweet-natured Gail was the one who ultimately held her interest and got the contract.

My mother used to drag my sisters and me to Manhattan whenever Gail had a casting call. Donna, Rayna, and I would stand off to the side with the stage-mothers and other peripherals as Gail joined the queue of picture-perfect children vying for a print ad or television commercial.

Once everything was in order, the agents, sponsors, and photographers would make their entrance. A hush would fall over the room as they paraded up and down the line of children, commenting recklessly on the talent.

"Such a shame about that nose…freckles are so passé."

Occasionally they would request a little dialogue and phrases like "Skippy Peanut Butter…yummy!" would ripple down the line, each child sounding as if Skippy was the only thing standing between them and death. If the sponsor wanted crying, tears would practically leap from tear-ducts. If coughs and sneezes were required, you would find yourself wondering why these boys and girls weren't home in bed. Even at their tender ages, these kids were pros.

And then, quite suddenly, would come the declaration.

"This one, this one, and this one," a lady wearing a pink Chanel suit and rope of pearls, her platinum blonde hair pinned up in a beehive, would say, pointing at each of the chosen children without making anything remotely approximating eye contact. It was exactly the way the judges pick their winners at dog shows.

I wished that one day the lady in the pink Chanel would look away from the beautiful children just long enough for her eyes to settle on me. I imagined her walking slowly and deliberately across the room, her eyes firmly locked on mine.

"Will you just look at this adorable little girl?" she would say to her assistant, probably someone named Bernie. "Where on the face of the earth has she been hiding?"

Bernie would just look up at the ceiling and shrug.

"What's your name, dear?"

"Linda Fingerhut. And I really do love Skippy Peanut butter."

Pink would shriek. "Oh. My. God. A voice like an angel. I must sign this child immediately."

The beautiful children in the queue would immediately develop pouty faces and the grown-ups would begin to murmur.

My mother would have a puzzled but pleased expression on her face. "Linda?" she would be saying to herself. "She wants Linda?"

"Are you thinking what I'm thinking?" Pink would ask Bernie in a stage whisper that could be heard all the way to the elevators.

"Bonanza?"

"Bingo! I think we can forget about holding that audition tomorrow afternoon. Little Linda here is exactly what NBC has been looking for. She'll be perfect as the crippled orphan girl who moves in with the Cartwright family. America, get ready to fall in love!"

When it became quite evident that Hollywood wasn't about to come knocking on my door, I found consolation in books. From the time we were babies, my mother read to us constantly: first nursery rhymes, then fairy tales, and later on from the brightly orange-colored Childcraft series. I got hooked early and hard. From the day I got my first library card until the day I went away to college, I was never without the four book maximum withdrawal. While a weekly trip to the library was part of our family routine, that schedule wasn't nearly enough to satisfy my addiction. After finishing my own books, I would be chasing down my next fix and invariably ended up reading each of my sisters' "baby" books as well. If books were considered a controlled substance, I would probably be spending most of my life in and out of rehab and making coffee at Bookaholics Anonymous meetings two nights a week. In any event, all those hours spent indoors in the company of books rendered me overly introspective and the only kid who returned to school after summer vacation without a tan.

Before my hometown abandoned the Revolutionary War era house that had served as our library for over a century in favor of an antiseptic modern structure, I spent many a Saturday afternoon tucked away in one of the library's irregularly shaped rooms. I went through stages, phases, fads. Once I read through an entire series of plays (*The Best of Broadway: 1941*, *The Best of Broadway: 1942*, *The Best of Broadway: 1943*; you get the idea). Then it was Shakespeare: comedies, tragedies, sonnets and all. My sophomore year in high school I plowed through Freud. I was spellbound by the case histories and hoping to glimpse something that would help to unlock the mystery of myself.

When I was ten years old, my mother broke with tradition and had her first son. The arrival of my brother Kenneth was nothing short of earth shattering. If you've ever heard the chorus "A son! A son! A son!" from the rock opera *Tommy*, you know exactly how we all felt. My mother had an adage: "Every girl should have a brother and a sister, and every boy should have a sister and a brother." True to her convictions, she went right ahead and produced her final child, my brother Jonathan. At the mature age of twelve, I felt more like a mother than a sister to these two little boys and to say that I adored them doesn't even begin to describe it. I can only imagine how thrilled my father must have been to have those two little bundles of testosterone in the house.

I do think that having six children created something of a dilemma for my parents, however. Being Marines, they were quite adept at matters involving scheduling and organization. But keeping track of the complex personality composition of each of their children may have proved too much. Perhaps it was for that reason, they deemed it necessary to assign each one of their daughters a single identifying characteristic. Linda was the smart one, Donna was the nice one, Gail was the pretty one, and Rayna had the personality.

I felt a shudder of recognition when I first studied Greek mythology and realized that there was a lot of history behind this kind of narrow character definition. Hermes thou art fleet of foot. Athena thou lucketh out with beauty. My parents were well intentioned, but being assigned one signature quality in childhood does have its downside. For one thing, having that single designated characteristic meant there were three other attributes that would be forever out of reach.

Did I mention we were Jewish? We were, as were most of the families in the town where I grew up, and so I was never subjected to dodging rocks or being called a Christ killer. But although we were the majority population in town, we adopted a minority mindset and I embraced the view that we were somehow simultaneously top dog and underdog. Being Jewish was apparently something to be desired and yet paradoxically resulted in being hated and despised by the world community.

While I never participated in any formal religious training, I received an education in Judaism nevertheless. My mother told me how Jewish people had been oppressed throughout history. She taught me about Hitler and concentration camps and how Jewish people were despised and reviled all over the world, sometimes even in America. She taught me that Jewish men made the best husbands ("they don't drink") and that it was important to support Israel ("we can always afford to send something"). She taught me that the Jews and Negroes always looked out for one another, because both groups knew what it was like to be hated. And above all else, she taught me to take pride in being Jewish.

My cultural understanding of Judaism was fairly idiosyncratic. For one thing, we kept track of all the Jewish actors, singers, musicians, and writers. Even those who tried to fly under the radar by changing their last names or getting nose jobs couldn't fool Betty Fingerhut. My mother, the former actress, had the inside scoop on every Jewish performer from Broadway to Hollywood. "Tony Curtis" my foot. But you didn't have to be a movie star to get caught in the glare of her discerning eye. We had a bead on all the families in town who went from Bromowitz to Brown ("it's easier to spell" they would insist) and any public figure whose nose appeared even a millimeter smaller after spending a few weeks on the Riviera was immediately suspect.

Then there was the food. Corned beef with mustard, never mayonnaise. Brisket and borscht, blintzes and knishes, gefilte fish and horseradish. But nothing compared with Sunday mornings. There would be bagels and lox, naturally, and cream cheese, with chives and without. These were accompanied by a full complement of bialys, whitefish spread, sable (the fish, not the fur; not that we had anything against the fur), Greek olives, and pickled herring. Every Sunday morning, fifty-two weeks a year, this was the drill. If I was lucky I got to ride shotgun with my father as he drove to Tabatchnik's or one of the other local Jewish delicatessens to pick up the spread. There is nothing more intoxicating than the fragrance of warm bagels and, invariably, two or three would mysteriously disappear on our way back to the house.

The theological aspects of Judaism were a little more slippery. My best friend in those years was a girl who lived directly across the street from me, named Sharon Sheffield. Between the ages of five and eleven, when my family moved across town to a larger house that could accommodate four growing girls and our baby brothers, I probably spent as much time in the Sheffield house as in my own. Sharon and I maintained 24 hour communication via two tin cans joined by a piece of waxed string which ran across the street and into our bedroom windows. If you pulled the string taut and spoke directly into the cans, you had a primitive but functional device by which to say important things like "Can you hear me?" and "Can you hear me now?" The fact that we could just as easily shout across the street to one another didn't deter us from the pleasures of our low tech phone.

Sharon and I had practically everything in common. We were alike in our love for the *Howdy Doody* show and our obsession with Barbie dolls. We had a shared passion for playing cops and robbers, cowboys and Indians, George and Martha Washington, and countless other invented games. Blonde (Sharon) and brunette (me) though we were, we considered ourselves to be virtually identical, apart from one essential, incontrovertible fact; my family was Jewish and hers was Roman Catholic. Although I didn't realize it until much later, the things I observed in Sharon's home informed my thinking about Christianity until I was twenty years old, driving and reinforcing my conceptualization of Judaism as the antithesis of Christianity.

Chapter 2:
Comparative Religion?

Throughout my childhood, the terms Christianity and Catholicism were synonymous in my mind. I was also aware of something called Protestantism, which I imagined to be a somewhat less virulent form of Catholicism. All other denominations, faiths, and philosophies were completely off my childhood radar screen. Religion was just some boring thing that grownups would occasionally talk about.

Back in the 1950s, childhood was a lot simpler. In the warm weather, all the kids in the neighborhood were outside playing kickball or flying kites. In the winter, we would insulate ourselves with mittens, scarves, puffy jackets, snow pants, and boots; you would find us sledding, ice skating, and building snow forts until dark. Back then, television was considered the height of space age technology. And watching TV was a less than sedentary activity; we would change the channel and adjust the volume by getting up, walking across the room, and turning a knob.

Back in the '50s, slingshots and spitballs were not unheard of. But teachers didn't have to worry about students pulling knives and children didn't have to worry about classmates with grudges carrying weapons of mass destruction. When there was a disciplinary problem, it was the kid who would be held responsible and not the teacher. And apart from someone being sent to the principal's office for a particularly egregious infraction, most misbehavior was effectively cured by the writing of "I will not do-whatever-it-was-I-did" one hundred times on the blackboard. In my grammar school days, when a teacher hugged a kid it was a good thing. These days it is likely to result in assault charges against the teacher and years of trauma counseling for the child.

By today's standards, my parents would have been considered negligent. Apart from Brownies, my only other extracurricular activity was taking dancing lessons. Five nights a week my father was relegated to driving back and forth across town, dropping off daughters and picking them up again at Miss Berry's School of Dance. As the classes were segregated by age, four girls meant four separate schedules. My nights were Tuesday and Thursday.

Tuesdays, beginning at seven o'clock, was ballet. I would arrive at class in a black leotard, black tights, and sneakers. Once there I would strap on my pink satin toe shoes and join the rest of the aspiring ballerinas in the traditional barre and port de bras exercises. After warming up, we would practice our routines, grande jete-ing and pirouetting to "The Waltz of the Flowers" and "Swan Lake."

"You sound like a herd of elephants," Miss Berry would bellow as we landed from our leaps with something less than elegance and grace. "Shoulders back, Linda," she would shout, words that were destined to follow me for the rest of my life. Tuesday nights at eight o'clock, I would go home, bandage my toes, and fall into an exhausted sleep.

On Thursdays, I'd spend that same hour in a snazzy red leotard, fishnet stockings and white tap shoes, busily tapping away to "Steppin' Out with my Baby" and "Puttin' on the Ritz." There is nothing quite like the happy, snappy, metallic sound of two dozen girls shuffling off to Buffalo in perfect unison. On those nights I would come home wired, the words "hop-shuffle-step, slap-stick, ball-change" skittering around in my brain like hyperactive children.

When my mother organized her daughters into a dancing quartet we achieved a modest measure of fame in town as The Thimble Sisters. We all loved performing and I can't help thinking that any little girl who hasn't had the opportunity to wear a sequined leotard and nylon net tutu has led a deprived childhood. The culmination of all our efforts was Miss Berry's annual recital, a true extravaganza, complete with costumes, stage makeup, and a live pianist. Each class would perform the routines they had been working on all year and Miss Berry and her daughter Andrea would do their annual "I Got Rhythm" dance and duet. It was not at all unusual for the Thimble Sisters to make a guest appearance at one of these affairs, soft shoeing across the stage to "Me and My Shadow." Afterwards, my parents would take us to Howard Johnson's for fried clams and milkshakes.

Dancing was something I enjoyed and so I stuck with it all the way through high school. After outgrowing Miss Berry, I took the bus into "the city" every Saturday morning, where I studied ballet uptown at the June Taylor Dance Studio and took jazz class at Luigi's on Broadway. If I had been more than halfway good at all this, I would probably have tried to dance professionally. Nowadays, the only dancing I do is the vicarious kind, mostly by watching movies. From *Saturday Night Fever* to *The Turning Point* to *Strictly Ballroom* to *Billy Elliot*, I love them all.

I don't want to leave you with an airbrushed and romanticized version of life in the '50s. People were no closer to perfect back then than they are now. And there was certainly plenty of bad stuff that went down. It just that the bad stuff was less pervasive than it is today and wasn't so endlessly reported, recounted, and rehashed in the public media. As a result, there wasn't a contagion effect that practically guaranteed that every bizarre act of rage would be endlessly copycatted from coast to coast. Children knew not to take candy from strangers, but they didn't have anything approaching the level of fear and suspicion that kids need nowadays just to survive.

Life was just slower. Oh, we had homework and we had chores, but we also had time to daydream. When we weren't practicing our dance routines or hunkered down in the family playroom, racing our silver trinkets around the Monopoly board, my sisters and brothers and I would occasionally have the great pleasure of doing absolutely nothing. And if we even dared to tell one of our parents "I'm bored," the response would either be "Why are you telling me?" or "Then do something!" We had been awarded full and complete responsibility for keeping ourselves entertained.

These were low-tech times indeed. I remember the day we got our first television set, a pint-sized black and white housed inside a massive mahogany cabinet. From the back of the television protruded a flat brown cord that my father stapled along the baseboard, up the wall, through the ceiling, and straight out to the roof. There it was connected to a highly unstable and chronically temperamental roof antenna that demanded frequent and delicate adjustments. At some point practically every day, my father would end up on the roof, risking life and limb, patiently trying to improve the reception on one of our three available stations. "It's good! It's good!" my sisters and I would shout out in unison, but by the time my father had climbed down from the roof, put away the ladder, and settled himself on the sofa, the picture would already be starting to roll. We all developed the dubious talent of following the itinerant picture on its endless expedition upward.

Even back then, too much television was considered a bad thing. I was lucky if my parents would let me watch two snowy, slowly revolving, thirty-minute shows a day. And, invariably, at least ten of those minutes would be spent turning the horizontal hold knob, sadistically situated in a shoulder wrenching location on the back of the set.

In the early days of television my sisters and brothers and I would sit on the floor, mere inches away from the screen, watching shows like *Mighty Mouse*, *The Lone Ranger*, and *Sky King*. Television viewing was very much a family event, quite unlike the solitary activity that is so typical these days. When Lawrence Welk's band played, we danced. When Mitch Miller's bouncing ball skipped across the screen, we sang. When Lucy shoved bonbons in her mouth, we laughed.

A few years later there arose some suspicion that deadly radar waves might be emanating from the sets and we were temporarily forced to watch *Get Smart* and *Sea Hunt* from clear across the room. That ended quickly enough and we all resumed our positions: stretched out on one of the couches, curled up in the vinyl recliner, sprawled out on the shag rug, or crunched into one of the bright yellow butterfly chairs.

But, radar or not, there was nothing on earth that could have prevented us from watching *The Ed Sullivan "Shew,"* which had something for absolutely everyone. I still remember the sweet scent of Dippity-Do wafting through the air on Sunday evenings as my sisters and I sat in front of the television set putting one another's hair up in rollers. There were ballerinas from Russia, acrobats from China, jugglers from Czechoslovakia, Topo Gigio from Italy ("Oh, Ed-deee"), and torch singers from practically everywhere. Mr. Sullivan even permitted a modicum of rock and roll, including Elvis, at least from the waist up. And we all know what happened when four boys from England debuted on his show on February 9, 1964. But what you may not know is what happened in the Fingerhut household that night.

Four Beatle boys, four Fingerhut girls; you do the math. It was quite evident that my sisters and I were destined to marry the Fab Four. All that remained was figuring out who would be tying the knot with whom. As my entire family sat in the den that Sunday evening, my sisters and I were ready to do battle. The rules had been debated, established, and ratified: a Beatle had to be on the screen by himself before he could be claimed and, once a sister made her declaration, all decisions were final. My parents and brothers had been sternly instructed to be as quiet as possible throughout the proceeding. This was extremely important because we had been forewarned that the Beatles had the potential to incite uncontrolled screaming any time they performed. We needed to be certain that our voices would be heard above the din as we laid claim to our husbands.

Donna, a well-known dawdler, picked this auspicious occasion for her one and only moment as the fastest and the first. "I call Paul" she shouted the second he appeared in close-up. I didn't especially mind the fact that good-looking Paul was out of the running as I was much more interested in mysterious George and irreverent John. But a few moments later when Gail shouted, "I call George," I began getting nervous, and a little annoyed, if you want to know the truth. There was something very unseemly about Donna and Gail being betrothed before their big sister.

But this was no time for philosophizing. If the cameraman didn't make his way to John very soon, I ran the risk of getting stuck with Ringo. I wanted desperately to go ahead and claim John, but rules are rules, and I waited, every nerve in my body on high alert, my heart practically beating out of my chest.

"I call John!" I shrieked the moment his face appeared, oblivious to the words "Sorry Girls, He's Married" when they subsequently flashed across the screen. And Rayna, no doubt grateful there was a remaining husband for her, was delighted to be left with Ringo.

Having completed our business, the four of us commenced screaming hysterically at the television set just like all the other young girls in America. Betty and Jerome Fingerhut looked at one another with the bittersweet realization that their little girls were going to be women sooner than they had imagined. Kenny and Jonny, apart from covering their ears to block out our screaming, couldn't have cared less.

"All my loving, all my loving, woo-ooo, all my loving, I will send to you." The future Mrs. John Lennon fell asleep smiling, dreaming of her husband and the life they would someday share. That night delivered a little bit of innocence and optimism to a nation that was still mourning the death of John Fitzgerald Kennedy, its favorite son.

As you can see, my childhood was remarkable only for things that most people would consider unremarkable. And what with all the activity of childhood, religion was a subject of general indifference. Nevertheless, there was a very precise consciousness of who was what.

This is who the Jewish people were. My immediate family, of course, and everyone in Israel. Then there were all my aunts, uncles, cousins, and grandparents; if there was a mixed marriage anywhere in my family tree I didn't know about it. As far as I knew, our genealogy was pure and uncontaminated all the way back to Abraham. More than half of the kids I went to school with were Jewish as were almost all of my friends.

And then there were the Jewish elite: Albert Einstein and Arthur Rubinstein and Leonard Bernstein and Albert Schweitzer. Not to mention Milton Berle, Henny Youngman, Jackie Mason, Joan Rivers, Jack Benny, George Burns and all the other comedians we would watch on *Ed Sullivan*. There were no Jewish criminals or dictators; in fact, all the Jewish people in the public eye appeared to be brilliant, creative, successful, and funny. The way I saw it, I was in pretty good company.

The Christians? Well, that was pretty much everybody else. First and foremost, there was the Sheffield family. Secondly, all the other families I ever saw on television shows or in the movies. JFK and Richard Nixon and virtually all the politicians and elected officials were Christians. Marilyn Monroe and John Wayne were Christians along with most of Hollywood. So were Billy Graham and Adolph Hitler, the Pope and Mussolini, Mother Theresa and the Boston Strangler. The Mormon Tabernacle Choir and the Lennon Sisters and the New York Yankees: all Christians, as far as I was concerned. Definitely a mixed lot.

The theological differences were quite clear. We prayed to one God: the God of Abraham, Isaac, and Jacob. Our God was alive and watching over us. He was a kindly old man with a beard who lived up in the clouds in a place called heaven. Our Jewish God dressed in a long white robe and spoke in Hebrew. The Christians prayed in Latin to a man named Jesus (presumably Catholic) who had died on a cross. The man's mother, father, and a ghost were also somehow involved.

As for actual religious practice, what it boiled down to was this. They had Christmas and we had Chanukah. They had Easter, we had Passover. Church on Sunday; temple on Friday. Catechism? Hebrew school. Confirmation? Bar Mitzvah. Turkey with mayonnaise on white versus pastrami with mustard on rye. It was as if Judaism and Christianity were two opposite but equal forces, mutually exclusive and somehow at odds with one another. For the most part it seemed monumentally irrelevant. In fact most of the year it was neither here nor there, a quintessential non-issue. And then there was Christmas.

Oh, how I envied the Sheffields. Outside their house, along the roof line, outlining the front door, and surrounding every window, were blinking, winking, Christmas lights, flaunting the fact that there was something magical, mystical, and thrilling going on inside that house. And the lights never lied. Every year the Sheffield living room would be consumed by a massive Christmas tree, scratching up against the ceiling, groaning under the weight of lights and garlands and ornaments, and presiding over mountains of presents promising even greater delights to come.

And, of course, there were the sweets. Mrs. Sheffield's kitchen was always in action, churning out endless batches of cookies which she would ice, decorate, and display like little Picassos, their scent filling the air with assurances of reindeer and sleigh bells and snowflakes to come. This was before the word "calorie" had made its way into the public lexicon and when a plate of cookies was placed before us, there was no holding back.

But the best, most Christmassy thing of all wasn't immediately obvious. It was located downstairs in the Sheffields' wood paneled basement, the purview of Sharon's big brother Dickie (who mysteriously morphed into an inscrutable creature named Rick when he turned fifteen). Down, down, down in the bowels of this mid-century home, down in the inner sanctum, down where the only windows were foggy little rectangles up near the ceiling, was the place where we were only allowed after the sincerest crossing of our hearts and fervent expressions of hopes to die if we so much as thought about touching a single thing.

Because at the bottom of those fourteen steps, perched above the swirling squares of almond-and-brown linoleum, was a miracle, a spectacle, and what I considered the defining element of Christmas: the Lionel train set. Although it's been forty-five years since I've seen it, everything is just as clear in my mind's eye as if it was on an IMAX movie screen. And while there is no description that can really do this justice, I will give it a try.

First of all, laid out on a massive piece of plywood were at least ten miles of train tracks set upon yards of cotton batting, folded and positioned to look exactly like snow. The train itself was a classic: a pitch black locomotive, ten little club and freight cars, and the reddest caboose imaginable.

Sharon and I would spend hours watching that train, listening to the haunting sound of its whistle, and imagining we were passengers traveling through that picture-perfect village. I can still remember the little headlights and the distinctive smell of the locomotive as it wound its way around the track, over a rustic bridge, through a mountain tunnel, past a train station, and around the corner of a tiny Main Street. Our hearts were on board as the train rushed past diminutive ice-skaters poised on a mirrored pond and circled through fields lush with stands of plasticized pine trees. Imagine a Currier and Ives Christmas scene transformed into a miniaturized winter wonderland and that was the Sheffield basement for the entire month of December.

Chanukah? Despite the very best efforts of my parents, it just couldn't compete. Christmas was without a doubt the superior holiday. And Christmas was the only time when I thought it wasn't all that great being Jewish.

But Christmas or not, there was something very disturbing about the Sheffield house. Something that unsettled me and reminded me I was in foreign territory every time I walked in the front door. It was the statues.

Now to be perfectly honest, I didn't really mind the ones of the lady. She looked peaceful and dignified and there was something poignant about the way she gazed at the baby in her arms. Inset into niches on the wall, perched on bookshelves, and positioned on credenzas, the lady was a silent, maternal presence practically everywhere in that house. Marble, wood, or bronze, she was equally serene in each incarnation. A little peculiar, but not a really a problem.

It was the crucifixes. In every room, on every wall, over every bed, over and over and over again, there was that tragic, bleeding man nailed to a cross. These miniature depictions of torture really frightened me. In fact, it felt so creepy to be alone in a room with a crucifix that whenever I visited Sharon, I would follow her around the house like a puppy. And when I finally got up the nerve to ask her about the statues, Sharon told me that the man was God and the lady was Mary, his mother. So, I thought to myself, the Catholics pray to a dead man and worship his mother, who had also presumably died. Our God, the Jewish God, was still alive. Christmas notwithstanding, maybe being Jewish wasn't so bad after all.

Chapter 3:
A Nice Jewish Girl Like Me

Actually, being Jewish was fine with me, at least as far as it went. The problem was that it just didn't seem to go far enough. As I moved into adolescence I began to appreciate the cultural and social implications of Judaism, but that was about the extent of it. I found myself preoccupied with the same questions that had intrigued me since childhood, but Judaism wasn't providing me with a single clue about the meaning of life, man's place in the world, or where we were all heading. And to be perfectly honest, there was more than just intellectual curiosity at work here. If I was going to be reincarnated, I wanted to do whatever possible to increase my chances of returning as the star of a Broadway musical and not a telephone agent for a collection company. Operating on the conviction that there had to be more to life than the temporal, material world, I spent most of my teenage years on the lookout for something or someone that would help me figure it out.

Don't get me wrong. I did give Judaism a bit of a whirl. Although my family didn't belong to a synagogue until my two younger brothers were old enough to attend Hebrew school, what with attending friends' and cousins' Bar and Bat Mitzvahs, I spent my fair share of time sitting (and standing and sitting and standing) in temple. At one point I was feeling cheated out of having received a Hebrew School education and my coming-of-age moment in the spotlight and I took it upon myself to attend Friday night services on my own.

There were two synagogues in my hometown; one was classified as reform (the liberal branch of Judaism) and the other was conservative (mid-way between reform and the stricter orthodox sect). I preferred the conservative temple, even though their services were conducted primarily in Hebrew, of which my vocabulary consisted mostly of: shalom. My affinity for this particular synagogue probably had something to do with the elaborate Oneg Shabbats that followed their Friday evening services; these were sumptuous buffets that would put many a wedding reception to shame. Scarfing down raspberry tortes, mini-quiches, and petit fours, I reveled in the gastronomical perks of my religion. From what I understood, the Christians celebrated their church-based activities with Spam and Velveeta sandwiches on Wonder Bread.

Going to temple was like entering another world, a quaint historical world steeped in tradition and ritual. I was entranced by the dignified appearance of the men as they donned their yarmulkes and tallits, instantaneously transforming them into old world scholars. I was dazzled by the bejeweled women, their heads stylishly adorned with the requisite hats, caps, mantillas, or lace kerchiefs, smelling deliciously of Chanel No. 5. I was spellbound by the haunting sound of the minor keyed music emanating from the sanctuary, signaling a wistful pathos that seemed to embody the very essence of the Jewish soul.

Unlike Christian services where the pastor faces his congregation, the rabbi led our worship of God by facing the front of the sanctuary and gazing forward at the ark, the chamber in which a copy of the Torah was nestled. Since the majority of the service was conducted in Hebrew, I would do my best to follow along using a phonetic prayer book provided for incompetents such as myself. I relied heavily on my peripheral vision to make sure I was standing and sitting at the appropriate moments, and tried not to get seasick from the multitude of men who were davening (a form of prayer characterized by a ritualistic, back and forth swaying motion).

After some singing and responsive reading, the Torah would be removed from the ark to be read aloud. At this point, the rabbi or his assignee, including the Bar-Mitzvah boy or girl on their occasion, would walk across the bimah (stage) and read the aliyah, or designated passage. This was a practice which not only permitted, but actually encouraged, the reader's Hebrew pronunciation to be corrected by the rabbi, who would use a feather-tipped stylus to direct the reader. After the aliyah was read, the Torah would be carried ceremoniously around the temple by the rabbi and a procession of elders. If you happened to have an aisle seat you would kiss the sleeve of your sweater (the men kissed the fringe of their tallits) and touch it to the Torah as it was whisked by. Then came the sermon.

As much as I enjoyed the pomp and pageantry, I had gone to temple in search of capital "T" Truth. But after the rabbi had delivered one of his earnest discourses, I would invariably find myself no closer to understanding the meaning of life than when he'd begun. It was kind of like getting a humanities lecture with a Jewish twist. There were instructive sermons about the sanctity of the Jewish family and the importance of the Jewish community. There were cautionary sermons about "mixed marriages" and the dangers of assimilation. There were inspirational sermons about the significance of the newly emergent Israel and our responsibilities as Americans. But while everything was interspersed with all the usual "love your fellow man" business, there was nothing that transcended the ordinary.

I never heard a sermon about God. It was all about tradition, ritual, ceremony, and liturgy; in a word: religion. And while there was plenty of that to be had, religion didn't seem to have a single thing to do with understanding any of the mysteries I was trying to unravel. The idea of actually encountering the living God in temple was beyond far-fetched. In fact, "God" was barely even in the vocabulary. From my point of view, temple was a decent enough place to hang out and have some refreshments but not a place to be taken seriously when it came to finding answers to the big questions. Judaism was an identity and a lifestyle, a culture and a community. But it just wasn't enough.

As I began high school I became interested in astrology. It was conveniently delivered to my house every day in the daily newspaper, plus it was fun. Over time, I graduated from reading my horoscope to diagramming astrological charts and making predictions based on which planet had stopped by which other planet's house for a game of Mah Jong. Even if it didn't all make perfect sense, well, at least it was in English. I went so far as doing a school project in which I devised a questionnaire attempting to identify my classmates' sun signs based on their self-professed personality traits. The signs of the zodiac became my signature doodle; while some teacher was droning on and on about the War of 1812, I was hard at work, hunched over my triple ring, loose-leaf notebook, sketching out increasingly elaborate renditions of those twelve signs.

Being a Gemini was great. Complicated, cerebral, creative, sensitive. Yep, that was me all right. Unbelievably, I could relate to every single character trait. I even felt strangely connected to domestic, nurturing Cancer, on whose cusp I was precariously perched, grateful that my primary astrological sign couldn't be mistaken for a major disease. But nagging away at the back of my mind was the reluctant acknowledgement that I could just as easily relate to the qualities ascribed to Scorpio. Or Aquarius. Or Capricorn. In fact when it came right down to it, I could pretty much see characteristics of myself in all twelve signs. There was such a strong element of subjectivity involved that eventually I saw the absurdity of the whole thing and realized that astrology boiled down to little more than an innocuous diversion. Or at least that's what it would have been, had it not led to other fields of inquiry. Astrology is sort of a "gateway drug" into the supernatural, the marijuana of the occult.

As my infatuation with astrology grew cold I started warming up to the more serious stuff. I figured the best way to learn about the afterlife was to have a little heart to heart talk with someone who was already on "the other side." I took to this like a fish to water and went from Ouija boards to automatic writing to séances, faster than you can say Edgar Cayce. I suppose I was drawn to the drama and mystery of it all combined with the hope that this would provide me with the answers I was seeking.

My interest and involvement in these pursuits waxed and waned throughout high school. At the time I was under the impression this was all enormously enlightening. But when everything was said and done, I was left with no more knowledge of the afterlife than I had to begin with. It could have been a lot worse.

By my senior year in high school, I had segued into what used to be called the "drug culture." I always considered that an odd pairing of words. I mean, it's not like there were social norms or generalized patterns of behavior that characterized everyone who ever took a puff or swallowed a tab. And it wasn't as if we were cultured, holding up our pinkies as we passed around a joint, saying things like, "Dahling, you simply must try this weed." But from the moment Dr. Timothy Leary advised my generation to "turn on, tune in, drop out," my world was never the same.

And why shouldn't the answers I was seeking be delivered via an altered state of consciousness? My religion had let me down; the world of the occult had let me down. This avenue to enlightenment made about as much sense as anything else. While I am not denying that there was a recreational element to my drug experimentation, there was a genuine inquisitiveness as well. Really!

And I did find the answers I had been seeking. Well, sort of. While under the influence of some tiny tablet I would invariably have a moment of spiritual clarity that seemed to wash away all the clouds of confusion and uncertainty, revealing the unadorned, unequivocal, ultimate essence of Truth.

Once it was *Sergeant Pepper*. Listening to those thirteen tracks was a crash course in enlightenment and the whole universe opened up to me as I listened to "Lucy In The Sky With Diamonds," "Within You, Without You," and, of course, "A Day In The Life." There were layers of significance and depths of meaning that went from the obvious to the esoteric to the enigmatic to the obscure. Unfortunately, the following day it all went back to being just a bunch of songs.

Another time it was my foot. A miracle of physiology. The key to the human body and the gateway to the divine. But only for a few hours.

Frequently it was a woven wool blanket, which would mysteriously morph into a manuscript completely covered in hieroglyphics. With chemical assistance I was able to identify these cryptic characters, but I was never quite able to decode them into language I could understand. This wasn't necessary a problem, however, because the hieroglyphics has a delightful manner of rising up from the blanket and performing charming little dance routines. This type of revelation is more commonly referred to as a hallucination.

Quite often it would be a word or phrase, which I would dutifully write down in order to preserve this knowledge for posterity. And many a morning, long after the chemicals had exited my system, I would find myself mystified by scraps of paper, covered in my own distinctive handwriting, declaring "the remainder of the reminder is the reindeer" or "the astral logic is presently past." What seemed like illumination at the time turned out to be nothing more than gibberish; there was the illusion of insight but without any genuine substance. It was the same deception that I had discovered in the world of the occult.

I poked my head into a dozen other dead-ends.

Scientology. I ran into some Scientologists my freshman year in college and was intrigued enough to read a book of science fiction penned by L. Ron Hubbard, the founder of the faith. I recall trying to master some strange disciplines, one of which involved making spiritual connections with people by staring directly into their eyes for extended periods of time. Although this kind of thing usually reduced me to laughter, I saw no reason why Truth could not also be funny. But the deal-breaker for me was when my Scientology friends started floating the idea that we were all God. For all the things I didn't know, the one thing I did know was that I most definitely was not God. Not even a little bit. I later learned that Mr. Hubbard had come up with the whole Scientology scam as a way to make money.

Socialism. Plenty of truth to sink my teeth into here. I was outraged by the oppression endured by the workingman. I was indignant at the unequal division of wealth. How terribly self-centered and nearsighted we were in America. Wasn't it evident that things needed to be shaken up and made right? I appreciated the good will behind the rhetoric but it seemed that every socialist I ever met was in desperate need of a toothbrush and a shower. Even Seekers After Truth have to be pragmatic and socialism was never going to provide me with the kind of man I could bring home to meet my parents.

Transcendental Meditation. Hey, if it was good enough for the Beatles, it was good enough for me. A little mantra went nicely with my tie-dyed t-shirts and bell-bottom jeans. And what's not to like about the sitar? But going deeper into myself wasn't necessarily a good thing, I soon realized. Plus, it was hard not to be skeptical at the prospect of achieving cosmic consciousness from a guru who was notorious for giggling.

The Koran. The Bhagavad-Gita. The I Ching. With each new initiative I would get excited and hopeful for a time and then invariably I would be disappointed. Sometimes I would come across misinformation or contradictions that would immediately put the kibosh on the whole thing. Sometimes there would be an oddity or inconsistency or some indefinable irregularity that gave me pause. Frequently I found elements of truth and wisdom. But always, there was a sense that something essential was missing. While these years of searching had yielded interesting bits and pieces of information, there was no belief system that seemed to offer that elusive, inclusive knowledge that I was intent on discovering.

Chapter 4:
Beantown Blues

You may wonder if at any point during my years of spiritual exploration I ever gave a serious thought to Christianity. The answer is: no. Not for a moment. Judaism may have turned out to be a bust, but I wasn't about to throw my support to the competition.

Besides, I thought Christianity was incredibly uncool. While Christians might have been a minority in my hometown, they were a highly visible one. My family lived just under the two mile limit that would have qualified me to ride the school bus. And so five days a week, ten months a year, for four long years, I walked past the local Catholic school on my practically-two-mile trek to and from high school. The sight of those poor St. Elizabeth's girls in their parochial school uniforms was pitiful. Starched white blouses, plaid skirts, oxford shoes, and knee socks; this was no way to dress back in the beaded, tie-dyed sixties. As for the nuns? If the highest female position in a religion called for poverty, celibacy, and bad fashion, I wasn't interested.

Furthermore, I was less than impressed with all the strange practices I had observed in the Sheffield home. Repeating a prayer while fiddling with a string of beads, crossing yourself every time you sat down for a meal, eating only fish on Friday -- it just seemed so superstitious. And then there were the creepier aspects of the religion, such as spilling your guts to a priest in a confessional and being expected to eat something that was supposedly flesh and blood. If I wasn't falling for all the Jewish mumbo-jumbo, I sure wasn't about to swallow theirs.

Even the name of their God was a problem. His first name, Jesus, had a soft sibilant sound that I always secretly liked. But his last name, Christ, was harsh and unpleasant to my ears. The "kuh" sound brought negative associations like the Ku Klux Klan, Concentration Camps, and Christ Killer. If I bothered to think about them at all, I pictured Mr. and Mrs. Christ as stern, authoritarian parents who had the unenviable destiny of watching their oldest son grow up only to be crucified. An Israeli Gothic couple with Addams family children. And I wasn't buying the part about Mrs. Christ being a virgin.

Everything about Christianity seemed weird or depressing to me. The painted velvet renditions of the Last Supper, the corny pictures of Jesus where his eyes followed you around the room, the ubiquitous crucifixes littering the Sheffields' walls. There was a somber, humorless element to Christianity that turned me off. I never read their Bible. I never went to any of their religious services. I never took the time to learn the difference between Catholicism and Protestantism. Why bother? It never even crossed my mind to take any of that sad, forlorn religion the slightest bit seriously.

Three months after my high school graduation, I started college in Boston with only the vaguest idea of what I wanted to be when I grew up. I decided to major in psychology, figuring that if I wasn't making progress discovering the meaning of life by looking outwardly, I might as well try looking inward. Besides, I figured that all the Freud I read back in high school would give me a head start.

The year was 1968. The country was mid-Haight-Ashbury, mid-Women's Liberation Movement, mid-Viet Nam. The draft was a constant roaring in our collective ears as one boy after another was shipped halfway around the world to a country none of us had even heard of a few years earlier. Despite the theoretical construct behind a random drawing of conscription numbers, everybody could see that the less educated, the less affluent, and the less connected were the ones destined to become heroes…or statistics. We baby-boomers did a lot of growing up as we watched the death count on the evening news and listened to the lies emanating from the White House.

Living away from home for the first time in my life, I found myself unconcerned with academics. I missed plenty of classes but never missed an opportunity to go to a concert or hang out at The Boston Tea Party, a pre-mega-venue rock club, now defunct. My college funded a Who concert and I saw them perform *Tommy* from beginning to end in our very own Student Union. I also recall going to see Jethro Tull, the Rolling Stones, and Donovan that year. I cannot remember a single class I took.

My girls-only dormitory was an old brick Victorian structure located in Kenmore Square, halfway across town from the main campus. Chestergate Hall was a true artifact, one of two remaining buildings in Boston with AC current. Or was it DC? I can never remember. Forced to use a battery-operated alarm clock, a battery-operated hair dryer, a battery-operated record player, and a manual typewriter, it was years before I took an electrical outlet for granted again. Each of the six floors in the dorm had its own unique blueprint and it was almost impossible not to get lost if you happened to lose count on your way up one of the creaky stairways. I'm not sure if there were actually stone gargoyles perched on the eaves of the roof or whether I just imagined they were there, but it was definitely that kind of place.

As gentlemen callers were not allowed upstairs, the first floor of the dormitory provided us with "date rooms," large, formal parlors featuring scarred hardwood floors, floor to ceiling windows, and Victorian lace moldings. These vestibules were decorated by Morticia Addams with moth-eaten Oriental rugs and furniture from someone's great-great-grandmother's attic. Everything smelled of dust and mold and even the stains had stains. When I wasn't out partying, I mostly kept to my fourth floor bedroom where I was permanently infatuated with the bird's eye view of the Citgo sign as it flashed hypnotically just outside my window. Unfortunately, the novelty of the whole plug-less thing quickly grew old.

I suppose some of my pharmacological investigation took its toll. Halfway through first semester I had lost any residual enthusiasm for academics. I had no particular career goals. In short, I was not motivated to do much more than attend the occasional class and hang out with my friends. The thrill of higher education, what little I might have had to begin with, was definitely gone.

On top of everything else, I was depressed. Not clinically depressed as in: can't eat, can't sleep, can't function. This was more of a low level sadness that permeated my entire being. I've since learned that the clinical term for this condition is dysthymia, a somewhat milder version of the more serious major depression, sort of a depression-lite.

In retrospect, I've come to believe that my dysthymia began in early adolescence. Of course back then I had no idea. I just assumed everybody felt sad all the time. I figured that pervasive feelings of despair and hopelessness were normal responses to all the pain and suffering in the world. And I further assumed that anybody who didn't feel that way had to be an idiot. Let's face it; with a war raging in Viet Nam, race riots breaking out all over the U.S., and kids high on acid jumping out of windows, who wouldn't be depressed? I didn't think there was anything the slightest bit unusual about the fact that I would lie awake night after night, worrying about practically everything. I thought that all of this unhappiness was just a natural part of the progression into adulthood.

As I got older, I began to realize that not everybody was like me. There were people who would go to bed at night, fall asleep, and wake up feeling refreshed the following morning. There were people who had something called "energy" and for whom daily functioning did not require constant monumental feats of willpower. And apparently there were even people who didn't feel the need to beat themselves up for all their shortcomings or feel a sense of personal responsibility for all the woes in the world.

Do you remember the first time you flew in an airplane? Were you the kind of person who needed to stay awake and attentive, alert to every bump and vibration in flight, convinced that without your full concentration the plane would be aerodynamically incapable of remaining aloft? Well, that's the way I was about everything. If I didn't worry sufficiently about my own personal problems, the misfortunes of everyone around me, the troubles besetting our country, and the evils being perpetrated upon mankind, everything would come crashing down. This is a responsibility that leaves a person feeling overwhelmed, drained, and exhausted. It left me feeling overwhelmed, drained, and exhausted. No wonder I was usually in a bad mood.

Midway through high school I began to realize there was something not quite right about all this and started to give some thought to seeing a psychiatrist. At that time, psychiatry was the only mental health profession I knew anything about. But going to a psychiatrist would have meant telling my parents and that, of course, was completely out of the question.

In those days seeing a shrink could only mean one thing: you were crazy. And being crazy meant being sent away to a funny farm, getting strapped into a straightjacket, and being hooked up to an electric torture machine. I decided things weren't that bad.

Well, perhaps they weren't, but neither were they getting any better. Now that I was away at college, I decided the time had come to do something about it. October of my freshman year, I made a call to the student health clinic and, after assurances of confidentiality, set up an appointment to see a psychiatrist. Finally, I thought, I'm going to get to the bottom of all this gloom and doom and learn how to be happy like everybody else.

I saw Dr. Aubrey exactly once. I remember the excitement stirring in my heart as I walked down Commonwealth Avenue that autumn day, thinking that now, at long last, there would be a solution to the misery that was me. The eighteen-inch fringes on my brown leather jacket flapped in the breeze as I marched purposefully and hopefully down the street. I was looking forward to the prospect of talking about my childhood and finally getting someone to understand how unfair it was that I had been stuck with a ten-thirty curfew, while all my sisters got to stay out until one o'clock in the morning. I planned to fill him in on the dressing-alike thing and all the fallout from the signature-personality-trait syndrome. I was hoping to spend many happy hours lying on a psychoanalytically correct sofa with my arms folded solemnly across my chest.

Walking down Comm Ave, I imagined myself freely associating while my fascinated psychiatrist was writing furiously, unable to bear the thought of missing a single significant word.

"Tree..." my psychiatrist would say, the tone of his voice slightly elevating as he pitched the word, his excitement barely contained beneath his salt-and-pepper beard, his fountain pen poised eagerly above a thick black binder.

"Mother," I would immediately respond, eyes closed, fully cooperating in this deep and dangerous exploration.

"Ahhh," my psychiatrist would reply, barely audibly. Clearly, he was impressed. I would hear his pen scratching out the letters: m, o, t, h, e, and r. This was the response that would set in motion the process that would eventually provide full and unobstructed entry into my subconscious mind.

"Yellow..."

"Mother."

My psychiatrist would be nodding almost imperceptibly as he recorded my response.

"Up..."

"Mother!"

"Excellent, Linda, excellent," my psychiatrist would whisper, his pen flying across the page, his breath coming in short puffs.

I was going to be good at this.

I was born to be analyzed.

In no time at all, I would become my psychiatrist's favorite patient. In fact, I would be a case that would hold such deep fascination I would need to be seen on a daily basis. Eventually my doctor would terminate treatment with all other patients so he could focus his full attention on the intriguing mystery of Linda.

Whenever I came in for a session, my doctor would have a pot of jasmine tea brewing and a dish of my beloved fruit slice candies resting colorfully on his credenza. With the gentle urging of my psychiatrist I would eventually agree to have our sessions viewed through a one-way mirror by psychiatric residents in training. There would be papers published. A television mini-series developed. Perhaps even a clinic established in my honor.

Oh, psychotherapy was going to be wonderful. I just knew it.

But Dr. Aubrey had an entirely different agenda.

His book.

My first and last psychiatric session began with me presenting a succinct and well-rehearsed summary of all my symptoms, along with an itemized list of my various idiosyncrasies, or what I used to call my "neuroses." The whole thing took about ten minutes.

Dr. Aubrey wanted to know if I was suicidal.

I was not.

Dr. Aubrey asked if he could read me a chapter from a book he was writing.

"I guess so," I replied politely.

Sitting in his office for the remainder of the hour, I went from confusion, to pride, to resignation. Confused as to why

I was listening to Dr. Aubrey and not the other way around. Flattered that he considered me worthy of the privilege of hearing his unpublished manuscript. And resigned to the fact that my problems were neither interesting enough nor serious enough to warrant his attention or treatment.

So this is psychiatry, I thought. No hope for me here.

I suppose I'm just destined to be miserable.

Chapter 5:
Then There Was Woodstock

Somehow I made it through my freshman year and back to New Jersey for what turned out to be my last summer in my parents' home.

Summer vacation was just beginning and the radio stations were touting a three-day, all-star concert in some obscure town in rural New York. I called Stephanie Karlen, a friend from high school, and we decided to go. The only glitch was going to be convincing my parents. This feat required several days of prolonged and strategic debate. My mother kept saying, "It's up to your father" and my father would say, "It's up to your mother." The divide-and-conquer technique worked perfectly.

My mother reluctantly agreed to let me take her Ford Country Squire on the condition I bring along my sister Donna. Her agenda here was for the two of us to bond and have a little sisterly fun, whilst Donna keep an eye on troublesome me, ensuring I didn't have too much fun. Although I never said anything to my parents about my countercultural activities, I think they must have suspected. For one thing, the rolling papers that my mother "accidentally" came across one day when she was rifling through my dresser drawers were probably something of a clue. And while I wasn't crazy about the idea of being slowed down by my kid sister, I realized it wasn't a bad trade off for getting the family station wagon.

So Donna, Stephanie and I hit the road for Woodstock. We were in high spirits, enjoying the ride, and making decent enough time until we hit some serious traffic. The New York State Thruway was eventually shut down by battalions of Volkswagen bugs and buses converging from all over the continent. But while the roads might have been clogged, there wasn't a bit of road-rage or honking of horns. In fact, the closer we got to Max Yaeger's farm, the more it felt like a massive family reunion. We could hear the whirl of helicopters, crammed with reporters and cameramen, circling overhead. The excitement in the air was palpable.

When we finally arrived at the concert grounds, ours was among the last cars allowed past the gates. In my rear-view mirror, I could see traffic coming to a halt as people who had been driving for days were being turned away. Once inside, we immediately realized there wasn't going to be anything even remotely resembling a parking lot. I ended up parking my mother's car on some sort of field and we settled in for the evening.

Then down came the rain. After spending the night in our little turquoise nylon tent, we awoke to a world bathed in mud. Stephanie immediately packed her knapsack and left. She decided she'd rather take her chances hitchhiking back home than endure one more unpleasant moment in the elements. But Donna and I were staying for the show.

For the next three days Donna and I woke up, washed up the best we could, and walked a half-mile or so to the concert area. Upon our arrival, we would survey the scene and prepare our line of attack. The fact that every square inch of land was covered with somebody else's bedspread or tarp didn't deter us in the least.

"Time to push our way to the front," I would declare determinedly to my sidekick. Every morning Donna and I navigated an obstacle course of humanity and settled down on our blanket, maybe fifty feet from the stage, where we were fortunate enough to actually see and hear the performers.

It has been said that if you remember the '60s you weren't there, and the same can probably be said about Woodstock. The best way to describe it all is to just recommend you see the movie. But here, admittedly with a little help from a couple of Woodstock websites, is what I've been able to recollect.

Richie Havens, who I had followed since I was in high school, opened the show. It was if he had been born for this one memorable moment, his twelve strings of "Freedom" ringing out across the fields. Later that day, Ravi Shankar, Arlo Guthrie, and Joan Baez took the stage.

Day Two brought Country Joe, who added a little politics to the proceedings. "One, two, three, what are we fighting for? Don't ask me, I don't give a damn. Next stop is Viet Nam. Five, six, seven, open up the curly gates. Ain't no time to wonder why, whoopee, we're all gonna die." This song had become something of an anthem in the anti-war movement, and singing along with Joe MacDonald were plenty of Handsome Johnnys who were sitting in wheelchairs or missing limbs. It was an angry, rueful chorus.

Later that day Carlos Santana kept things moving along with his band and bandana, his fingers wringing one euphoric note after another from his guitar. Then there was Canned Heat and their eight million amps churning out "Going Up The Country" and "On The Road Again." Creedence Clearwater Revival performed one hit song after another, half a million people accompanying John Fogerty on his earnest, distinctive vocals. And Janis Joplin, an amazing, heart-breaking talent, did her set.

There was also a little band called The Grateful Dead, revered by their army of devoted, tie-dyed followers. I'd never been a Deadhead and had always been a little put off by the heavily-haired, heavily-sedated adherents of Mr. Garcia. But, not surprisingly, the Deadheads, who spent their entire lives following the band all over the country, were by far the best-prepared attendees. Seemingly within minutes of their arrival, they were completely organized, with barbeques grilling, clotheslines hanging, and their children happily playing. I recall them being kind and generous and going out of their way to help people who were suffering psychedelic distress.

I remember the sense of disconnect when Sly and the Family Stone took the stage. After a series of mostly white performers in t-shirts and jeans, the group's colorful costumes and shiny black Afros put them in sharp contrast. I think they were the only performers who had any kind of choreography and they did a tight set, notable for a spirited rendition of "I Want to Take You Higher." They were followed by Jefferson Airplane and The Who.

Day Three. Joe Cocker started things off, followed by Ten Years After, The Band, Johnny Winter; Blood, Sweat and Tears; Crosby, Stills, Nash and Young, and the Paul Butterfield Blues Band. Pretty much your average concert lineup.

There were many others. Much to my regret and the decades later dismay of my sons, I didn't actually see Jimi Hendrix. By the time he took the stage, my sister and I were exhausted and had long since returned to our tent. But the sound of Hendrix's guitar traveled effortlessly through the dense summer air and I remember lying on my sleeping bag listening to "The Star Spangled Banner" being played like some kind of revelation.

Woodstock held many firsts for me. It was my first time sleeping under the stars in a tent. Not that I actually saw any stars, but still, it was a far cry from my bedroom or my dorm room, the only other places I had ever previously slept. I discovered that on a rainy night it was folly to even touch the inside of a nylon tent as water would immediately come dripping in. But, all in all, it was still kind of fun.

It was my first time seeing naked people. At nineteen, I was what used to be called "a good girl" and my virtue was quite intact. At that time, the other major female classification was "nice girls," and I'll leave it to you to figure that one out. In any case, there were people walking around naked. Male and female, young and old, day and night, there they were. I remember feeling kind of embarrassed for them and averting my eyes when I saw one walking in my direction. I felt somewhat guilty for exposing Donna to all this unexpected flesh. And I was hoping like crazy that my mother wouldn't find out.

It was my first time using a Port-a-Potty. Well, sure, plenty of people were doing their business in the woods, but I felt it necessary to hold on to some vestige of civilization. As I waited in line to use the Port-a-Potty for the first time, I was imagining a somewhat scaled down version of the powder room in my parents' house. Given the size of the structure, I didn't expect there would be a shower or bathtub, but I certainly counted on such basics as a sink, mirror, and toilet seat. Not to mention, an exhaust fan. Was I ever in for a surprise.

I developed a technique whereby I would hold my breath for as long as possible and then hold my t-shirt up against my nose when forced to take a breath. I also developed a technique whereby I never again went camping.

Another first: the first time I ate "vegetarian." Of course, I'd eaten plenty of vegetables in my time. As a matter of fact, I've never had a vegetable I didn't like. But this was something different. It involved tofu and strange flavors and spicy seasonings. It also seemed to result in an increased need to stand in the Port-o-Potty line. But as this was what was available, this is what I ate. All the food was free. I imagine it was donated by someone who had a heart and realized there would be plenty of kids from New Jersey who would be traveling without sufficient supplies. Quite unlike the Woodstock '97 event, during which bottled water went for eight dollars a pop and everybody was looking to make a buck.

Well, while Donna and I were having ourselves a grand old time enjoying what turned out to be the iconic event of our generation, my mother was seething in suburbia. She passed those three interminably long days immobilized in front of the television set, watching the news coverage of half a million hippies smoking pot and, yes, walking around naked. This was not the show to which she had entrusted me with the care of my naïve, innocent little sister.

I subsequently learned that she had tried to have us paged. Picturing my sister and myself being forced to shoot heroin by deranged rock-and-rollers, my frantic mother had called the New York State police, making up a story about my father having had a heart attack. She insisted that the Woodstock organizers be notified and that we be located at once.

"May I have everyone's attention please? Will Linda and Donna Fingerhut, come to the front desk immediately. Your father has had a heart attack and your mother would like you to call home." In the highly unlikely event we were ever actually paged, we never heard it. In any case, when my mother couldn't reach us, she began calling hospitals and morgues, fully expecting to be told that, yes, they had two unidentified teenage girls with long brown hair and wire-rimmed glasses lying lifelessly on marble slabs.

Three days later when Donna and I arrived home, my mother fell upon my sister with kisses and tears and glared at me with an expression that would shatter rock. Anybody from my family knows the look I am talking about; the rest of you probably have someone in your family who has a similar gift for barely-contained fury. Staring wordlessly at her mud-splattered, wood-paneled, terminally contaminated Ford Country Squire, my mother turned her back on me, wrapped her arm protectively around my sister, and led her poor traumatized daughter into the house.

I was left to find my way into the house entirely on my own.

The moment the front door opened we were assaulted by the aroma of brisket of beef, Donna's favorite meal. My mother sat Donna down at the kitchen table and served her plate after plate of the steaming beef and vegetables. There were tears in Betty Fingerhut's eyes as she hovered over her second-born, all the while shooting the evil eye over at me, terrified that precious Donna might never recover from this terrible ordeal.

I was relegated to feeding myself.

Of course Donna had just had the time of her life but, in a family with six kids, we all knew enough to soak up a little extra parental attention when we had the chance.

My mother did not speak to me for two weeks. She put all of her theatrical training to excellent use as she heaped love and affection on Donna and the other favored siblings while acting as if I was invisible. Acting as if a family member was invisible as a means of punishment was a regular part of our family repertoire. Fortunately, by this time, I was old enough to think it was funny.

I tried reminding my mother that "the quality of mercy is not strain'd," but she wasn't having any of it. It turned out my mother was quite willing to dish out Shakespeare when it suited her purposes, but wasn't the slightest bit interested in being on the receiving end of the Great Bard.

As the summer wore on, my mother gradually got over her anger at me and came to realize that I was not personally responsible for single-handedly arranging the defining event of my generation in a deliberate attempt to scare her half to death and corrupt my little sister. She did, however, feel compelled to sell the station wagon.

When I went back to Boston in September, I had no idea that this was going to be the year when I would meet my future husband, drop out of college, and find God.

Chapter 6:
On the Road

I was greatly relieved when sophomore year provided entry into an electrified 20th century dorm situated directly across the street from the Student Union. This was a modern, Meet-George-Jetson structure, comprised of three towers, two of which housed co-eds, the other, our prospective husbands. It was in the shared lobby between the men's tower and one of the women's towers, that I met the young man I was to marry.

I met "Bill" in October of 1969. It was a Saturday night and my roommate Linda and I had just spent several hours over in the men's tower, listening to music with Robbie Kuddish, a friend from my hometown. We were on our way back to our room in the "B" tower when we decided to stop and spend a few minutes in the lobby.

And, yes, my roommate's name really was Linda. Believe it or not, when we were introduced to people, it was not unusual for someone to ask if we were twins. Amazing. First of all, we looked absolutely nothing alike. Secondly, and more to the point, why would anyone possibly think parents would give their twin daughters the same name? Shades of the quadruplet nonsense I endured as a little girl. Of course, Linda and I thought this was hilarious and forthrightly admitted to being twins any time we were asked. Upon confirmation of this discovery, the genius would nod sagely, declaring, "I knew it."

As Linda and I sat talking that night, from the corner of my eye I noticed a tall young man with the most impressive Afro I'd ever seen on a white boy. A few minutes later when I glanced ever so nonchalantly around the room, I saw him looking steadily in my direction. I pretended not to notice as Bill inched his way across the lobby, going from one Naugahyde bench to another, until it was practically impossible not to acknowledge him. I thought he was cute and shot him a little smile. Bill immediately came over. We then embarked upon a conversation that would continue for another seventeen years.

From the very beginning, there was a connection between the two of us. There was chemistry and commonality and a sense that we were somehow destined to be together. While I was more inwardly directed, Bill was more politically minded and had an evolved social conscience. In record time, we fell in love and joined forces in figuring out what was going to be the basis of the life we intended to share together.

(Although Bill was an important presence in my life in the succeeding seventeen years, each of us had our own subjective

experience of the events I am about to describe. And while some of the story that follows could be described in terms of "we," in the interest of simplicity I'll stick with the first person.)

This was one of those proverbial turning points, the veritable fork in my road. By this time I had essentially given up on learning anything of real value in college and so, for all intents and purposes, had dropped out. It was more of a default thing than an actual decision. When you skip enough classes, miss enough tests, and end up with a grade report covered with incompletes, it kind of dawns on you that you have probably crossed a line.

But none of this mattered any more. I was in love! There was a new element, a new understanding, a new way of interpreting the world around me. The sky was bluer, the world was truer, the whole universe seemed to be smiling. Invigorated by this emotion, I reviewed all my previous experiences, considered everything I believed to be true, and threw it all into one final, ultimate equation. And from that monumental effort, there emerged a Belief.

It was fundamental.

It was radical.

It was the Capital "T" Truth that had so far eluded me.

It was the meaning of life, the purpose of mankind, and the key that unlocked every mystery in the universe.

It was Love!

This was an epiphany beyond explanation. A discovery beyond definition. From that moment on I committed my life to love. Loving Bill and loving mankind. What higher calling? What deeper direction? What loftier aspiration?

Well, it all started out pretty well. Every person who came across my path provided an opportunity for kindness, unselfishness, and compassion. No judgment, no discrimination, no criticism, nothing but love for the waitress, the clerk, the passenger on the subway, my guy. How simple! How basic and yet how revolutionary! The Beatles were entirely correct when they said love was all we needed. This revelation was so powerful it virtually catapulted me out of Massachusetts.

I flew out to Los Angeles. Confident in manifest destiny, I arrived at LAX with optimism brimming in my heart and the Mamas and Papas' "California Dreaming" playing non-stop inside my head. After quickly exhausting my limited funds I ended up getting picked up hitchhiking by the pastor of an African-American church in Compton, a section of L.A. better known as Watts. Watts had barely survived an extensive period of rioting and block burning the year before and by the time I arrived it looked a lot like a war zone. Reverend Simms, no doubt amused by the do-gooder rhetoric emanating from the backseat of his Lincoln, challenged me to put my money where my mouth was by loving some of the brothers and sisters in his congregation.

And that was how I ended up living in the back room of a church thrift shop in post-riot Watts with the ashes still smoldering on the sidewalks. Within a matter of days this twenty-year-old Jewish girl from New Jersey had her first fulltime job. Mornings, I would arise from a lumpy mattress and wash up in the phone-booth-sized bathroom that serviced both my room and the rest of the thrift shop. The remainder of the day would be spent laundering, ironing, and tagging bags of donated clothing. Evenings, I would heat up a can of Spaghetti-O's on a hot plate, watch TV on a 17" rabbit-eared black-and-white, and try my best to keep my distance from the resident rodent. I felt fully alive.

And for about two months, that was the way it was. Monday through Saturday, I worked my fingers to the bone. But on the seventh day? It was there in Watts that I first set foot inside enemy territory: church. And it was nothing at all like I expected.

Keep in mind; practically everything I knew about Christianity I had learned from my childhood friend Sharon, but this church was most definitely not Catholic. There weren't any crucifixes. There weren't any statues. There weren't any priests or nuns. In fact there was nothing the slightest bit somber about this white stucco edifice, centrally positioned on one of Compton's main thoroughfares.

Every Sunday morning, scores of African-Americans would meet and greet each other like long-lost friends and then file into the brightly lit sanctuary, which bore an uncanny resemblance to my junior high school assembly hall. Dressed in their Sunday finery, the congregants would settle into the pews, filling the church with their lively chatter and laughter. And at ten o'clock sharp, when the choir started to sing, well, I would defy even the most melancholy misanthrope to sit still. The music was just what you would expect in an African-American congregation; *Sister Act*, only for real.

As for Reverend Simms' sermons? Could that man preach! Loud and proud and well lubricated by the flow of "amens" and "glorys" emanating from the congregation. Week after week I heard him preach with fire and conviction about ethnic pride and the importance of family in the Black community. He preached about social injustice and our responsibility as Americans. He preached about doing good and loving your fellow man. I don't remember him saying a whole lot about God. In fact, apart from the hymns, God didn't really appear to be a part of the proceedings.

Hey, wait a minute. This was all starting to feel pretty familiar. Church was just like temple, only with better music.

So, this is Protestantism, I thought. Well, what do you know.

I was more or less accepted by the churchgoers who looked on this white college dropout from the east coast with a combination of curiosity and cynicism. That was good enough for me because being even a peripheral part of this community was immensely interesting and gratifying, at least in the beginning. But as I got to know these people better, they gradually evolved from being a corporate entity, easy to love in some abstract, impersonal fashion, to being a bunch of imperfect individual human beings with all the annoying, aggravating qualities to which we are all heir. Not so easy to love after all.

In fact, some of them were downright impossible to even like. And I tried. I smiled and struggled not to complain as I went about sewing missing buttons on shirts and ironing donated dresses. I tried my best to overlook it when someone was less than thoughtful or even unkind. When someone was cold or rude toward me, I gave them the benefit of the doubt, gritted my teeth and loved them anyway. I tried like crazy to love those inconsiderate, self-centered people who didn't seem to appreciate the fact that I was three thousand miles from home, laboring full-time in what was essentially a sweatshop, and receiving only the most meager room and board in return. But it just wasn't working.

This was something I hadn't considered. When I came up with the Love theory, I assumed that having made up my mind, I would simply be able to go ahead and do it. How was I to know that some people were inherently unlovable?

Plan B. I would love the nice people, the deserving people, the people who loved and appreciated me. With all the people in the world, that alone would keep me busy, so no need to stress out. But sooner or later, even the nicest people are liable to have an off moment and it was only a matter of time before everyone had hurt or offended me in some way.

And then the final blow. I began to experience moments, hours, days even, when I was less than enthralled with the guy who had gotten me started on all of this love business in the first place.

Oh, no. This was bad. All that certainty, all those good intentions, right out the window. I still believed Love was the answer. But exactly how to love was the question.

I had no Plan C.

Time to move on. I packed up my suitcase and headed north.

Chapter 7:
What Happened in Santa Cruz

When I left Los Angeles, I headed toward the only other city in California I knew anything about: San Francisco. This was a couple of years after the Summer of Love, but I was pretty sure that if I could make it to Haight-Ashbury there had to be at least a few lovable people left with flowers in their hair. Although I was discouraged by my inability to love everybody in Watts, I had high hopes for the rest of the state. So my thumb and I headed north to the City by the Bay. Keep in mind, in those days hitchhiking was a less than death-defying way to get around. Half a dozen rides later I was about sixty miles south of Santa Cruz.

By the time Carl and Penny pulled over in their emerald mist Buick Skylark I was tired and hungry and more than relieved to climb into the back seat next to their three-year-old daughter Monica. And when the sun started slipping into the Pacific and they invited me to have dinner and spend the night at their house, I gratefully accepted. After an hour or so of vehicular conversation, I was feeling safe and comfortable being with Carl and Penny and figured it was unlikely I was in the company of murderers, what with the little girl and all.

As we followed one winding Santa Cruz road after another, the driveways grew progressively longer and the houses began getting farther apart. And from every direction, there emerged a lushness of trees. Majestic redwoods presiding over the landscape. Solemn oaks standing guard as far away as the eye could see. A pervasive quietness seemed to engulf us as we slowly wound our way upwards, the darkening sky barely visible through the leafy branches. It was like being inside a fairy tale and I wouldn't have been the least bit surprised had I seen Little Red Riding Hood or Hansel and Gretel skipping along somewhere in the distance. By the time we arrived at Carl and Penny's little house I was completely disoriented; I'm sure I couldn't find my way back to that house today if my life depended on it.

The house itself was a humble three-bedroom ranch with hardwood floors and rustic furniture; nothing fancy, nothing you'd ever see in *Elle Décor* or *Metropolitan Home* magazines. There was no television set, no stereo, nothing to distract from the beauty of the surrounding nature. After two months in the back room of a thrift store in Watts, this cozy little house felt like a luxury suite at Trump Tower. As Carl and Penny went about preparing dinner, there was no fear, no sense of: uh-oh, what are these people up to? There was just a deep, profound, abiding sense of peace.

What was it about these two? There was something different about this couple, something perceptible and yet indefinable. I observed them closely as we sat around the dinner table eating something I thought was chicken and only later learned was rabbit. Carl was an average-looking guy, pleasant and personable, entirely unpretentious. Penny was an attractive but unassuming woman wearing simple clothing, no make-up, and not a single piece of jewelry. Monica was affectionate, chatty, and definitely her daddy's little girl. There was a warmth and kindness that characterized everything Carl and Penny said and did, and which didn't seem the least bit artificial or contrived. Watching them, listening to them, I wanted what they had.

Later that evening, after the dishes were cleared and the scraps were added to the compost pile (something I'd never seen before; must be a California thing, I thought), we sat in the living room and began the discussion that was about to change my life.

I asked them to tell me about themselves.

"We're Christians," they responded.

Shouldn't have been a big deal. I had met Christians before, in fact had just spent the past two months almost exclusively in the company of Christians. I had even attended their church. But for some strange reason, immediately and inexplicably, all the air went out of the room.

Suddenly and quite unexpectedly, I felt very defensive, very guarded, and very, very Jewish. I wanted to spin a dreidel, dance the hora, eat a dozen knishes, and then go shopping at Bloomingdale's. Time to put an end to this conversation.

"Well, I'm Jewish." Never had these words felt truer than at that very moment.

"Did you know that Jesus was Jewish?"

Well, sure. My mother had explained that to me back when I was a little girl. She had taught me that Jesus was a great man, kind of like Moses and Buddha and Gandhi and Winston Churchill. I just figured that somewhere along the way Jesus had parted ways with Judaism and started his own religion.

"Yes, I know. But I'm not too big on organized religion. What people want to believe is their own business."

"Oh, but Christianity isn't about religion. It's about having a personal relationship with God. To do that you have to be born again."

Aha! Now I get it. They're Born Agains. I'd heard about these people before; back then they were also known as Jesus People and Jesus Freaks. I knew all about these self-righteous religious fanatics and their exclusionary, narrow-minded, right wing propaganda. But Carl and Penny didn't seem that way at all. In fact, they seemed to be entirely sane and not the least bit judgmental.

It was then they told me their stories. They told me how their lives had been quite different a few years earlier, how Penny had been a fashion model in New York City and how Carl had been a financial consultant. They told me how they had been living the fast life, caught up in ambition and materialism, their marriage perched precariously on the rocks. Then they described the changes that had occurred when they had each "accepted Jesus as their Lord and Savior," whatever that meant.

I was moved by their openness and their honesty. They weren't making themselves out to be superior human beings; if anything, it was quite the opposite. But more than that, I was impressed by their conviction. It wasn't a matter of: well, this is something we think might be true and we've been considering it for quite some time and it seems to make sense. Instead, they were talking with absolute certainty about an experience that had transformed and revolutionized their lives. And they were talking about having a "personal relationship with God," something that had to be hubris, a psychotic delusion, or a possibility beyond anything I had ever considered.

"Have you ever read the New Testament?"

"Ummm, I don't think so." I'm thinking: what's the New Testament?

"It describes who Jesus was and what he did and how he fulfilled the Old Testament prophecies about the Messiah. Maybe it's something you'd be interested in reading so you can decide for yourself?"

Not exactly a hard sell.

On the one hand, I was thinking, if these two want to pray to the dead guy on the cross that was their business, but I would just as soon stay out of it. On the other hand, I had to consider the remote possibility that they might be onto something.

And so I figured, why not? I'd never had any qualms about reading any other book, so what did I have to lose by reading this New Testament of theirs? They seemed so sincere that I thought it was the least I could do given the fact of their hospitality. It was just a book after all. A depressing one, no doubt, but just a book.

So later that same night there I was, lying in a bed, in a room, in a house, on a mountain, with three people I didn't even know ten hours ago sleeping soundly just down the hallway. In my hands was a big, black, hardcover King James translation of the Bible. It must have weighed five hundred pounds. The New Testament they had directed me to read was about two thirds of the way into the book. I stared guiltily at the page dividing the two sections. Centered on the page in mammoth letters were eight words: "The New Testament – Words of Christ in Red." So this was where Judaism ended and Christianity began.

I felt like a traitor. Visiting a church, listening to gospel music, talking about religion, all of this could be dismissed as just passive exposure. But making the choice to read this book, this Christian Bible, was a deliberate step of disloyalty. I felt like I was betraying my family, betraying the American Jewish community, betraying the entire nation of Israel. I felt like I was disrespecting all the Jewish people who had lost their lives in the Holocaust. It felt like an act of religious mutiny.

I was immobilized. I didn't want to commit this act of treachery but at the same time I kept asking myself, suppose Carl and Penny are right and all this is true? Do I want to miss out on something so important, so critical, and just because of some personal hang-up? I decided that this was an occasion that called for prayer.

Prayer was something unfamiliar to me. Oh, there were a few prayers I had memorized in synagogue, but they were in Hebrew and I didn't know what they meant. Then there was the "Now I lay me down to sleep" prayer, but that didn't seem appropriate for the occasion either. And so I just talked to God. Out loud. And as close to verbatim as memory will allow, this is what I said:

"Dear Jewish God, if all of this is real and if Jesus really is the Messiah, please show me. Amen."

Then I took a deep breath and began reading the Gospel of Matthew, a first-hand account of the life of Jesus, written around 40 A.D. by a Jewish accountant. It took a while to accustom myself to the archaic language of the King James translation, but as chapter followed chapter something strange began to happen. There was a growing conviction in my heart that what I was reading was not a fantasy, not a fable, not a myth, and certainly not a fairy-tale. I can't explain how or why but I had an intuitive sense that every word I was reading was true. There was something about this book that just felt different than the Bhagavad-Gita or Koran or any of the other religious literature I had previously read. It felt alive.

And then there was Jesus. He was nothing at all like I expected. The dour, somber, angst-ridden guy that I had always imagined was instead a man of compassion and conviction, filled to overflowing with…well, with life. Jesus was unlike any religious figure I had ever read about or studied. He was unlike any literary or historical figure I had ever read about or studied. I was surprised, intrigued, and completely caught up in the story of this man.

The more I read, the more I understood why people were so drawn to him. There was something in how he turned a phrase, told a story, used language in such a way as to give it multiple layers of meaning. There was something in how he conducted his life, cared so deeply for the people with whom he associated, was full out obedient to doing the will of God. Jesus could be gentle or stern, allegorical or direct, joyous or sorrowful. He was fully present in every moment and yet his eyes were always fixed on something up ahead.

I could see that it hadn't exactly been smooth sailing. As Jesus traveled throughout Israel, teaching and healing, gradually revealing who he was to his followers, he infuriated the religious establishment by exposing their hypocrisy. The Pharisees, a Jewish sect that believed in literal interpretation of the Jewish Bible, were incensed when all their attempts to trap Jesus were thwarted by his superior understanding and application of Scripture. They were further outraged when Jesus referred to God as his Father and applied the Jewish Scriptures about the Messiah to himself. By Chapter 26, Jesus had made the religious establishment so uncomfortable that they made up their minds to do him in.

I didn't really have a problem believing the parts where angels suddenly appeared, food mysteriously multiplied, and people were miraculously healed. My foray into the world of the supernatural had already convinced me that there was a whole lot more to life than the physical, material world. Plus, it just made sense to me that God, who created nature, would have power over it.

The problem I had was in knowing what was coming. And what Jesus apparently knew was coming as well. The tragedy. The end. The cross. I felt a knot in my stomach as Jesus made his way into Jerusalem and straight into the trap that was set for him by Judas and the chief priests and elders. All this brilliance, this radiant life, was rapidly, inexorably coming to an end. I felt my heart beginning to break because I too had felt drawn to him. In fact I was beginning to think that Jesus might actually be who he said he was. I didn't understand why he was destined to such a terrible end.

I felt sick to my stomach when I read about the crucifixion. The detail and specificity of Matthew's account made me feel like I was watching from behind a pillar as Jesus was humiliated, tortured and ridiculed. Why did this have to happen? I just didn't get it. Jesus had lived a life of uncompromising obedience to God. He had spent his life in service to others, never harming another person, never breaking a single law. And here he was, being subjected to the vilest punishment imaginable. Nailed to a cross. Dead and destroyed.

And then I turned the page.

You may find this hard to believe, and I am somewhat embarrassed to admit it, but I had never heard anyone say that Jesus had risen from the dead. The only images I had ever seen of Jesus were of him lying in a manger, seated at Da Vinci's *Last*

Supper, or nailed to a cross. Nowhere, anywhere, had I ever heard about a stone rolled away from an empty tomb and an angel with a message that has echoed through the centuries.

He's alive.

Chapter 8:
Just a Book

Dead or alive, Jesus was nothing like I had imagined him to be. All of my preconceived ideas about Christianity suddenly seemed immature and ill informed. But as taken as I was by the Jesus I was reading about, I was just as appalled by the whole idea of Christianity. There was nothing about this offensive religion that appealed to me in the slightest. And I was horrified at the thought that belief in Jesus might require me to affiliate myself with this alien organization. Was I going to have to start collecting Hummel Christmas ornaments? Making pilgrimages to the Vatican? Spreading Hellman's on my sandwiches instead of Gulden's? Converting to Christianity would be the ultimate defection.

But the question just wouldn't go away. Suppose Jesus really was the Messiah? I needed to figure out for myself whether or not Jesus was who he claimed to be. And what, if any, bearing this might have in my life.

As Carl and Penny didn't seem in any rush to get rid of me, I settled in for a period of exploration and reflection, glad to have a comfortable bed and some decent food for a change. Still, I struggled mightily with a powerful sense of disconnect between the man I had read about in the Gospel of Matthew and everything I had ever believed about Christianity up until this time.

Floating through my mind were images of some of the atrocities I had heard about when I was growing up. And more than once, I challenged Carl and Penny regarding the morality of their faith.

"What about the pograms?" I asked indignantly. "How can you justify the way Christians persecuted and murdered Jewish people all over Eastern Europe and Russia? Did you know that they 'baptized' Jewish infants by holding them under water until they stopped breathing?"

"Not everyone who claims to be a Christian is necessarily a Christian," they would reply. "Followers of Jesus would never do such a thing."

"Then tell me about the Nazis," I would demand. "Tell me how six million Jews were humiliated, tortured and gassed while the whole Christian community stood by. Why would I even consider a faith that had the most notorious anti-Semite in history in its camp?"

"God loves the Jewish people and real Christians feel the same way," they would respond. "There were many Christians who risked their lives to help Jewish people in those terrible days. But granted, there were many more who didn't. This was certainly not Christianity's finest hour."

And then, invariably, they would come up with some biblical quotation regarding the Jewish people and Israel.

"The Bible says, 'I will bless those who bless you, and whoever curses you I will curse; and all the peoples on earth will be blessed through you.'" (Genesis 12:2-4)

"The Bible says, 'As you have been an object of cursing among the nations, O Judah and Israel, so will I save you, and you will be a blessing.'" (Zachariah 8:13)

"The Bible says, 'Whoever touches you touches the apple of his eye.'" (Zecharaiah 2:8)

The Bible, the Bible, the Bible. Everything always came back to the Bible. What was the big deal about this big book?

And just in case you're wondering whether I'm talking about the Jewish Bible or the Christian Bible, the answer is: both. This is an important point, because it was the connection between the two that sealed the deal for me in terms of believing there was any validity to either one of them.

Everyone has an opinion about the Bible and, even though I had never read it, I had an opinion as well. I thought the Bible was innocuous religious literature comprised of elements of history, philosophy, and mythology. I considered it impossibly vast, overly complex, and excruciatingly boring. And I didn't need a big black book to tell me that I was supposed to knock off my bad behavior and fly right.

The Jewish Bible was written between 1440 and 400 B.C. Over the centuries, trained scribes copied and recopied the Scriptures, as they were known, by hand until the advent of the modern printing press. The first five books of the Jewish Bible, sometimes referred to as the Pentateuch or the Torah, are attributed to Moses. The other thirty-four books are written by numerous others, including: Kings David and Solomon, prophets Isaiah, Ezekiel, and Jeremiah, and the mysterious, yet prolific, Uncertain.

My own personal knowledge of the Jewish Bible consisted of the 23rd Psalm and a handful of stories plucked from Genesis. And now, quite suddenly, there was an entirely new Bible to consider. Since I knew next to nothing about my own Bible I questioned the morality of investigating the competing version. But if I was going to make an informed decision and put this issue to rest, once and for all, there didn't seem to be much choice in the matter. It's just a book, I reminded myself. Just another book.

I subsequently learned that the Christian Bible was comprised of both the Jewish Bible (which Carl and Penny referred to as the Old Testament) and an additional text, called the New Testament. The New Testament was written between 55 and 95 A.D. It was written primarily in Greek, although portions were written in Aramaic, the language most widely spoken at the time. I was surprised to learn that it was written entirely by Jewish people who had observed all the commotion that occurred two thousand years ago when a young Jewish man went around healing lepers, raising the dead, and turning the whole religious establishment on its ear.

The first four books of the New Testament, often referred to as the Gospels, are narratives of the life of Jesus, who was known as Yeshua back then. The Gospels of Matthew, Mark, and John are first person accounts of what the writers observed during the three years they traveled with Jesus, during his public ministry. Luke, a physician, based his book on reports by various eyewitnesses. If you've ever heard even two people describing the same event, you know how different one person's recollection can be from another's. And yet, amazingly, there is no conflict or contradiction between any of the four accounts of Jesus' life, even though they cover an extensive period of time, provide much detail, and were written from varying perspectives.

Quite a few of the remaining twenty-three books of the New Testament are attributed to a man named Paul. Paul, a Pharisee (sort of the equivalent of an Orthodox Jew) and highly respected member of the Jewish establishment, had been vehemently opposed to the idea that Jesus might be the Messiah. In fact, Paul was notorious for tracking down and killing Jewish believers until he, too, was transformed by a personal encounter with Jesus.

While I had considered myself a decently educated and well-read individual, at the age of twenty, I had never read a single page of the Christian Bible. I had explored astrology, Scientology, Buddhism, and the occult. I was up to speed on transcendental meditation and was well acquainted with the epiphanies endemic to psychedelia. I had no issue when it came to studying the Koran or the works of Edgar Cayce. But when it came to the Christian Bible, I had a problem. Thanks, anyway. Thank you so very much. But believe me, I did not want to read about that dead guy on the cross. The very thought of it was beyond depressing. Nobody, and I mean nobody, was more surprised than me when Carl and Penny convinced me that there might be something remotely relevant in that big black book.

By this time, I was convinced that Jesus was someone who could not and would not be ignored. His true identity was something that had to be resolved, one way or another, before I could leave Santa Cruz and get on with my life.

As I made my way through the New Testament, the words continued to come alive and resonate in a way that was unprecedented for me. There was no doubt that Jesus was slowly capturing my heart. But as I continued reading, it was the references to Old Testament prophecies as they were being fulfilled in the New Testament that grabbed hold of my intellect. I could not come up with any rational, alternative explanation for how words that were written over a thousand years before the birth of Jesus could be so specifically fulfilled. I could think of no reasonable explanation except to believe that the Old and New Testaments were books with supernatural properties. Books that revealed the capital "T" Truth that had eluded me for so long. Books that were inspired by God.

As I followed one trail of footnotes and cross-references after another, I was amazed to learn that the Jewish Bible was far from a book of philosophy and rules. And to my surprise, it had a lot to say about the Messiah; in fact there are probably hundreds of references to the Messiah embedded in the Old Testament. What follows are just a few of the prophecies that got my attention, further convinced me that Jesus was who he said he was, and helped me get over my hang-up about Christianity being…well, Christianity.

Micah 5:2-3
But you, Bethlehem Ephrathah, though you are small among the clans of Judah, out of you will come for me one who will be ruler over Israel, whose origins are from old, from ancient times.

I had always pictured the "little town of Bethlehem" as a Christian settlement. Turns out it was Jewish. It would appear that someone hailing from this village was to have a pretty remarkable destiny. And I certainly hadn't heard of any other notables claiming Bethlehem as their birthplace.

Isaiah 7:14
Therefore the Lord himself will give you a sign: The virgin will be with child and will give birth to a son, and will call him Immanuel.

I had thought all that virgin business was entirely a Christian invention. Well, I supposed, if God could create the electron, the solar system, and everything in between, placing the Messiah in the womb of a virgin was well within his supernatural capacity. By the way, Immanuel means "God with us."

I have since discovered that there are some who object to this interpretation, insisting that the Hebrew word "almah," which is most frequently translated as "virgin" can also refer to a "young girl." Here is where common sense and logic come in. Why would there be anything noteworthy about a young girl conceiving? And how could such an ordinary event possibly be considered a sign? It is exactly that, the very miracle of a virgin conceiving and giving birth, which makes this event remarkable enough to warrant recording.

Proverbs 30:4
Who has gone up to heaven and come down?
Who has gathered up the wind in the hollow of his hands?
Who has wrapped up the waters in his cloak?
Who has established all the ends of the earth?
What is his name, and the name of his son?
Tell me if you know!

I had been taught that the idea of God having a son was anti-Jewish. But apparently King David knew of his existence and was only waiting to discover his name.

Isaiah 9:6-7
For to us a child is born, to us a son is given, and the government will be on his shoulders. And he will be called

Wonderful Counselor, Mighty God, Everlasting Father, Prince of Peace. Of the increase of his government and peace there will be no end. He will reign on David's throne and over his kingdom, establishing it and upholding it with justice and righteousness from that time on and forever.

Again with the son. I had always thought this son business was in direct contradiction to Judaism. In this passage I saw how one particular son was destined to be called Mighty God and Everlasting Father. When Jesus said "The Father and I are one" and "If you have seen me you have seen the Father," some considered this blasphemy. Here I could see that those statements were consistent with the prediction of the Jewish prophet Isaiah.

Zechariah 9:9
Rejoice greatly, O Daughter of Zion! Shout, Daughter of Jerusalem! See, your king comes to you, righteous and having salvation, gentle and riding on a donkey, on a colt, the foal of a donkey.

This didn't mean much of anything, in and of itself. Except when I considered the fact that in the New Testament I read that Jesus' entry into Jerusalem just prior to his crucifixion was on the back of a donkey.

I had been under the impression that all the Jewish predictions of the Messiah had him wearing a crown and riding a white horse. And some Old Testament verses do in fact characterize the Messiah as a powerful conqueror, one who brings peace and justice as he restores the city of Jerusalem and establishes his kingdom on earth.

Over the centuries, there have been Jewish scholars who believed there would be two separate Messiahs, one a "Suffering Servant" and the other a "Conquering King." The New Testament reveals the concept of a single Messiah who will come twice.

> *Psalm 22: 7-8, 16-19*
> *All who see me mock me; they hurl insults, shaking their heads: "He trusts in the Lord; let the Lord rescue him. Let him deliver him, since he delights in him." Dogs have surrounded me; a band of evil men has encircled me, they have pierced my hands and my feet. I can count all my bones; people stare and gloat over me. They divide my garments among them and cast lots for my clothing. But you, O Lord, be not far off; O my Strength, come quickly to help me.*

This one really got my attention. The entire psalm provided a vivid description of crucifixion approximately one thousand years before this method of execution had been devised. It also provided a wealth of other information specific to the crucifixion of Jesus.

Isaiah 53:2-6

He had no beauty or majesty to attract us to him, nothing in his appearance that we should desire him. He was despised and rejected by men, a man of sorrows, and familiar with suffering. Like one from whom men hide their faces, he was despised, and we esteemed him not. Surely he took up our infirmities and carried our sorrows, yet we considered him stricken by God, smitten by him, and afflicted. But he was pierced for our transgressions, he was crushed for our iniquities; the punishment that brought us peace was upon him, and by his wounds we are healed. We all, like sheep, have gone astray, each of us has turned to his own way; and the Lord has laid on him the iniquity of us all.

There was an emotional truth about this passage that made me feel as though I was looking straight into the heart of God.

Isaiah 53 offered a picture of the Messiah as one who would suffer and die, making atonement for the sins of mankind. Once. And for all. Kind of like an eternal Yom Kippur. And along with the rest of the book of Isaiah, it provided a view into the character of God.

Zechariah 12:10

And I will pour out on the house of David and the inhabitants of Jerusalem a spirit of grace and supplication. They will look on me, the one they have pierced, and

> *mourn for him as one mourns for an only child, and*
> *grieve bitterly for him as one grieves for a firstborn son.*

I realized that this prophecy had yet to be fulfilled in its entirety. There are still many Jewish people who continue to believe that Jesus was a liar, a magician, or a fraud. Or who dismiss him as having been a great man or a prophet.

I didn't remember hearing any of the above scriptures being read at any time when I was in a synagogue, although it's possible they might have been...in Hebrew. I definitely didn't recall any these prophetic passages being discussed. Back in 1970 when I began to read the Bible, both parts of it, for myself, I discovered connections I could not dismiss or ignore.

But so what? These could all be coincidences. Or maybe Jesus and his followers contrived these situations in order to trick people into thinking that prophecies from the Scriptures were being fulfilled. Or maybe none of this even happened.

All I can say is that, in combination with all the other things I was seeing, hearing, and personally experiencing, I was becoming increasingly convinced. That God was who he revealed himself to be in the Bible (both parts) and that Jesus was in fact the Messiah.

Chapter 9:
Lady Liberty

It was getting harder and harder to do so, but still I held back. Years of spiritual dead-ends made me think twice, and twice again, about jumping to any premature conclusions. I kept waiting for the deal-breaker, the moment of exposure, the point where I would see the duplicity of these people and the folly of their faith. But while I certainly saw imperfections in Carl and Penny, these only reinforced the need for a belief system that freely acknowledged the shortcomings of creation while providing continuing access to the creator.

For the second time in my life I was faced with the prospect of going to church. As I wanted to accumulate as much information as possible in order to make an informed decision, I decided I might as well give it another shot. So on Sunday mornings I joined Carl and Penny's family on their drive out to a little white clapboard church that would have been right at home on the set of *Little House on the Prairie*.

The church, which was affiliated with a strict fundamentalist denomination, harbored beliefs and practices that were on the extreme end of conservativism. They believed in a very literal interpretation of the Bible and practiced a lifestyle that bordered on asceticism. The church permitted no dancing or secular music. The women all wore their hair long, eschewed makeup and jewelry, and were sanctioned from wearing any type of clothing considered to be masculine, including pants. The men were similarly restricted and discouraged from wearing wedding bands, watches with metallic bands, or "worldly" clothing, like leather jackets or blue jeans. There was no watching of television, no going to movies, no reading of secular literature. They didn't even chew gum.

This church boasted no organ or choir, just a rinky-dink piano and a stash of dog-eared hymnals. While hymns were unfamiliar to me, I felt drawn to the depth of the words and ageless beauty of the melodies. And whatever the singing may have lacked in technique, it more than made up for in volume.

Unlike the synagogues I had attended, and unlike the church I had visited in Watts, God was an almost visceral presence in this place. The minister talked about God as if he knew him personally. While he didn't have an abundance of polish or charm, there was a conviction and authenticity in his sermons that I found powerfully persuasive.

Church wasn't just a Sunday morning affair. People stayed in touch throughout the week, frequently helping one another out in any number of practical ways, from sharing produce from one another's gardens to running errands for shut-ins. The level of personal investment that I observed and that took place with very little fanfare impressed me. This was a community of people who truly cared about one another.

Over the next few weeks, my conflictual feelings at reading the New Testament gradually lessened and I found myself in a focused and objective frame of mind. While I had not yet completely made up my mind about Jesus, I was quite certain that the New Testament was more than just another book. But before jumping ship, shouldn't I at least take the time to learn a little more about the vessel I was about to abandon? I decided to give my own Bible, the Jewish Bible, a fair shot. Time to get back to my roots, I thought. And this is what led me to another remarkable discovery.

My sister Gail and her husband Rob have a picture hanging in their den that is made up entirely of green, blue, and silver dots of varying sizes. When you enter the room, this print looks like an abstract work of art. But if you stand directly in front of it and stare at it in just the right way, something interesting happens. The dots begin to emerge and recede and the next thing you know you are looking at a three dimensional picture of the Statue of Liberty.

It took me a while to learn the knack of seeing the picture within the picture, but now that my eyes are trained, I can immediately see straight through the dots to Lady Liberty. The uninitiated can stare at those dots till the cows come home without ever seeing what's there, never knowing there is more going on than meets the eye. But the only way to get to that point is to spend however long it takes staring straight at the print, un-focusing and re-focusing your eyes, until the magic happens. And once you learn to see it, it becomes impossible not to.

As I began reading the Jewish Bible, the Old Testament, I had a similar experience. On the surface, it was nothing more than a collection of stories, a book of history, a religious treatise, seemingly intended to encourage people to lead moral lives by adhering to some principles of conduct. But that was just the top layer, the blue and green and silver dots. Because hidden within the Old Testament, just below the surface, concealed within the text, I discovered something else entirely. It was Jesus. Chapter upon chapter, verse upon verse, he was all over the place. Not only in the prophetic passages I had discovered earlier but in innumerable, less obvious places. I was amazed and mystified as Jesus kept emerging unexpectedly from all over that ancient Jewish book. And after a while, it became impossible for me to not see him.

I followed him throughout the book of Psalms. He was all over the book of Isaiah. Everywhere from Genesis through Malachi there were scriptures revealing and confirming the Messiah-ship of Jesus. What were clues and signposts at the time they were originally written were now confirmation and verification that Jesus was who he claimed to be. The reality of Jesus virtually jumped out at me in the same three-dimensional manner Lady Liberty emerged from her frame.

Right from the beginning. In the beginning. "God said, 'Let us make man in our image, in our likeness'" (Genesis 1:26). What was meant by this pluralization of God?

Again and again, God is recorded as having interposed himself in our world. In the book of Genesis, "the Lord God was walking in the garden in the cool of the day" (Genesis 3:8). Throughout chapters 17 and 18, God appeared in physical form to Abraham. In chapter 26, he appeared to Isaac. In chapter 32, Jacob wrestled with a man, who subsequent verses clearly characterized as a manifestation of God. In the book of Exodus, chapter 33, God spoke "face to face" with Moses. In the book of Daniel, chapter 3, Shadrach, Meshach and Abednego were observed walking around unscathed in a furnace with a "fourth like the Son of God."

That so-called Christian idea of the incarnation, God appearing in human form, was turning out to be pretty Jewish.

I was willing to consider that this might be true but wondered how it was even possible. I came to realize that time does not exist for God in the same way it does for us. People move horizontally through time, always existing somewhere between yesterday and tomorrow. God is operating on an entirely different plane. One that is horizontal, vertical, and multi-dimensional in ways that we cannot comprehend.

I realized I was approaching a make or break point. I had to either embrace this new knowledge or reject it. I could imagine walking away from Santa Cruz and all that I had experienced there. I could imagine never seeing Carl and

Penny again and never setting foot inside another church. I could easily imagine setting aside all the rules and regulations that were attached to this particular denomination. But what I couldn't bear was the thought of walking away from Jesus himself. What it all boiled down to was this: either Jesus was the Messiah or he wasn't.

I had put the request out to God. "If Jesus really is the Messiah, show me." And the more I read the Bible, the more I understood the answer. I already knew that I was a sinner...I just never realized that I needed a savior. My eyes were opened to the realization that if I wanted to have a relationship with God, both in this world and in the next, it would have to be on God's terms.

And the day came when I just knew. I believed Jesus was the Messiah. There was an intuitive, emotional realization when I read the New Testament. There was a logical and intellectual understanding when I examined the Old Testament. There were no holes or inconsistencies or contradictions in what I was studying, as had been the case in every other belief system I had explored in the past. This was the Truth I had been seeking for as long as I could remember. "For God so loved the world he gave his one and only Son, that whoever believes in him shall not perish but have eternal life" (John 3:16). I was convinced.

I didn't need Carl and Penny to tell me that passively believing all this wasn't going to be enough. This was a revelation that called for a decision and a commitment. So, to the extent I was able, I counted the cost. Virtually everybody

I was close to was Jewish. I knew that a decision to accept Jesus as my Messiah would not exactly be celebrated by my sisters and brothers. Undoubtedly, it would be ridiculed by my friends.

But it was my parents I was worried about. I was pretty certain my parents would see my belief in Jesus as an act of defiance and defection. Throughout my life I had heard of Jewish families who would disown a family member who "converted." They would break off all communication, act as if the person had died, and sometimes even hold a funeral service. This kind of extreme reaction was a possibility that chilled me to the bone. I realized I was running the risk of permanently alienating my parents and putting the rest of my family relationships on the line as well. But it was a risk I would have to take.

I made the decision to follow Jesus. I asked God to forgive my sins, take control of my life, and help me become the person he wanted me to be. Amen.

And then it was like awakening from a very long dream, discovering the life I had been living up until then was only half a life, and entering into a whole new dimension of understanding and experience. It was like being born again.

Chapter 10:
If I Were God

Following my encounter with God, I headed back to Boston with the intention of spreading the good news up and down the eastern seaboard. As I had spent the first twenty years of my life never hearing a single word about Jesus being the Messiah or about God's plan of salvation, I quite reasonably assumed that this information had yet to be disseminated east of the Rockies. I decided to make it my business to get the word out.

It didn't take long before I discovered there were Christians of the Santa Cruz variety all over the place. Even Jewish ones like myself. Back in Boston I met some people from a group called Israel's Remnant, an organization similar to Jews for Jesus. Every Tuesday evening the group would meet in the Boston suburb of Brookline for Bible study, discussion, and prayer. At any given time there were from a dozen to upwards of fifty people in attendance. Before long, I was one of them.

It was wonderful getting together with people who shared both my background and my beliefs. And it was a tremendous relief to realize I was not alone. No longer feeling like a traitor, I learned how to integrate my newfound beliefs into my identity as a Jewish person.

I had always operated under the assumption that you were either Christian or Jewish, but that you had to pick one or the other. It was no more possible to be both at the same time than it was to simultaneously support both the Yankees and the Red Sox. But here were people who considered themselves fully Jewish, by means of their heritage, culture, and genetics, and fully Christian, by means of their acceptance of Jesus as the Messiah. It wasn't that complicated.

I learned that not all believers were as literal in their interpretation of the Bible as had been the case in Santa Cruz. There are some basic beliefs that are common to all Bible believing Christians, primarily the need to accept the sacrifice of Jesus to obtain forgiveness of sin. Beyond that, each denomination has its own particular ideas regarding worship and lifestyle. There are certainly more beliefs that believers hold in common than those that separate them; however, as I heard different perspectives, I no longer felt it necessary to adhere to the strict practices prescribed by Carl and Penny's church.

Israel's Remnant, for which I subsequently worked for two years, was dedicated to helping other Jewish people come to the same knowledge and understanding that we had found. We spread the word about Yeshua Ha Mashiach (we called him by his Hebrew name) using any means at our disposal: handing out tracts, performing street theater, even making unscheduled appearances in synagogues to speak with rabbis. As you can imagine, not everybody appreciated our efforts. Ignorance of scripture and misconceptions about the Messiah are endemic in the Jewish community. We were seen as rebels and insurgents. Life was exciting.

Bill, the young man I had met in college, had an experience parallel to mine and ended up coming to the same conclusions. To say that my family and Bill's were less than thrilled by our faith in Yeshua would be the epitome of understatement. Interestingly, Bill's family accused me of pressuring Bill into "converting," whereas my family blamed Bill for manipulating me into this act of betrayal. As Bill and I were both Jewish, the logic behind this kind of thinking was somewhat flawed. Thankfully, neither family disowned us, as we had both previously feared. We tried our best to walk the line between honesty and sensitivity and somehow managed to preserve our family relationships while still maintaining our personal integrity.

Bill and I were married. In my hometown synagogue, with both of our families in attendance, I repeated my wedding vows phonetically in Hebrew. It wasn't until many years later that I learned what it was that I had promised. As things turned out, it was more than I delivered.

While I didn't expect my friends and family to necessarily embrace my newfound faith, I wasn't exactly prepared for some of the harsh judgment I encountered. Even today, there is no lack of criticism and stereotyping when it comes to Christianity.

Christians tend to take a bad rap. We are frequently looked upon as idiots and bigots. How can anybody with half a brain not believe in evolution? How can anyone avoid being cynical in the face of convenient jailhouse conversions? Who wants to be associated with a religion that purportedly hates gay people? I myself cringe when I turn on the "inspirational" television station and witness so-called ministers of God: one selling vials of holy water, another scraps of cloth, still another promising untold riches to viewers who "plant seeds" by sending in hefty donations.

It is perfectly OK to be a recovering alcoholic or addict of any variety, but Christians are characterized, and sometimes even caricatured, in ways that range from slightly offensive to downright insulting. Unfortunately, there are more than enough Christians in the public eye who have fallen from grace to fuel and reinforce the pejorative view of Christians as liars, hypocrites, or worse. And who can deny that over the centuries there have been terrible atrocities committed by people claiming to be Christians? That is a sad and incontrovertible fact. But real Christians don't go around exterminating people in ovens or burning crosses on people's lawns. Indian pacifist and human rights activist Mahatma Gandhi was quoted as saying, "I like your Christ; I do not like your Christians. Your Christians are so unlike your Christ." A sad commentary.

It is said that Christians aren't perfect, just forgiven. I can only express my sadness that people fitting some of the above descriptions have shaped many people's views on Christianity. However, I do believe there are a far greater number of professing Christians who are conducting their lives in ways that are worthy of admiration and respect.

There are also quite a number of understandable reservations about believing in a God who allows his creation to endure so much pain and suffering. A God who created a world where injustices so often prevail and where depravity is increasingly commonplace. A God who created a planet in which the elements seem to be at war with the inhabitants. In the battle of intellect versus faith, it is easy to understand why people are reluctant to embrace a belief system that doesn't make excuses for a world that is saturated with woes.

If I were God things would be very different. For starters, I would have designed the world so it would never rain on the weekend. Summer would bring heat, but not humidity, and everybody would have a summer cottage on the body of water of their choosing. In autumn, leaves would remain on trees until the very last moment, when they would flutter gracefully through the air and disintegrate just before touching the ground. In winter, snow would paint the landscape a shimmering white, while immediately melting on streets and sidewalks. And Spring? Well, spring would be exactly the same as it is now.

With me as God, you could be sure there would be no cruel earthquakes, no rampaging tornadoes, no tsunamis destroying villages, no hurricanes tearing up towns. There would be no more crumbling coalmines or unpredictable nuclear power plants; we'd get all our energy directly from the sun. Animals would be content to live peaceably within their respective habitats and birds would know better than to do their business on windshields. Nature would be a charming, docile force, imbued with beauty, elegance, and restraint.

When it came to creating people, I would have taken an alternative approach as well. Everyone would be overflowing with love, kindness, and generosity. People would spend all day knocking themselves out being nice to one another. They'd be funny, too, and have plenty of personality. If there were such a thing as an argument, it would be over whose turn it was to give the other one a foot rub. No lying or looting, no backbiting or bribery. No anti-Semitism. No pedophiles. You would sleep well each and every night without a moment's worry about whether or not your kids were alright. In the morning you would leave your house without even thinking about locking the front door. People would fall in love and marry the person of their dreams, remain ridiculously in love throughout their lives, and die simultaneously in their sleep at a ripe old age. Assuming they have to die at all.

What else? Oh, no diseases, of course. Watching my friend Kate battle ALS over the past three years has convinced me that it would be A-OK to dispense with everything from the common cold to cancer. And no mental illnesses, either; no psychosis, developmental disabilities, or mood disorders. There would be moods, of course. They would cover the entire spectrum, from serenity all the way to bliss. No anger, guilt, anxiety, or sadness. And why would there be? We'd all be looking at the world with twenty-twenty vision, smiling at each other with perfectly aligned, cavity-free teeth, and eating all the pasta we wanted while maintaining our ideal body weight. Everyone would be fit as a fiddle and there would be no such thing as a bad hair day.

In my position as God, I would ensure that houses would remain structurally sound from the moment the foundations were poured. Basements would stay dry, roofs would never leak, and electrical systems would never need upgrading. Everyone's home would indeed be their castle and you could call in the team from *Divine Design* or *Extreme Home Makeover* any time you got the urge to redecorate. Money, if there were such a thing, would never, ever, be a concern.

Wish you had a plasma TV? I'd see to it that you had one delivered and installed within the hour. That diamond tennis bracelet you've had your eye on? I'd have it gift-wrapped and waiting for you at the jewelry store, along with some matching earrings. Getting tired of driving your old clunker? In no time flat I'd have you behind the wheel of that Ferrari, Beamer, Audi TT, or whatever it is you've been obsessing about since you rode your first Big Wheel.

As you can see, I would be a kind and benign God, a supreme and gracious Higher Power who really "gets it." Every single day I would do anything and everything necessary to make sure it was all going smoothly for each and every one of you. I would be a God with a big heart and an even bigger wallet, a God who would do whatever it takes to keep you happy.

But, as you have probably figured out, I am not God. And things are not even close to the idealized version of life detailed above. Instead of spending our days skipping merrily across the meadow and being served gourmet dinners on the beach at sunset, most of us are working fifty plus hours a week trying to make ends meet and don't have a single relationship that couldn't use some improvement.

But think about it. Would you really want to live in the sterile, sanitized world I have described? Would having everything so immediately and predictably available make them less meaningful? Would it really be all that wonderful if everyone was walking around as if they'd been lobotomized? Would never having to worry about your kids be a satisfactory trade-off for a shallow, superficial existence?

What I'm getting at here is the concept of free will. The idea that we are designed to be thoughtful, reflective creatures with the ability to make choices. And make them we do, some good and some not so good. Over the centuries, the decisions of mankind have resulted in biological, psychological, and environmental consequences, and so we find the world in its present state. But one decision we never had to make was whether or not to have free will. That was already determined by our creator. The real God.

And so things are the way they are. Sometimes wonderful, but much of the time, not so great. People don't always exercise their free will in a kind and compassionate fashion. Furthermore, nature isn't nearly as serene and well behaved as we would like. So not infrequently we find ourselves asking,

"How could a loving and merciful God allow _____?"
Here, of course, is where you fill in the blank. And the longer
you live, the more you realize there is no shortage of ways to
complete that sentence.

So what does all this mean? Is God unkind? Indifferent?
Unaware? Dead? Or maybe there is no God? Maybe you concur
with the big bang theory or have some hypothesis of your own
about how we all ended up here drinking lattes, shopping at
the mall, and surfing the web.

I don't think these questions are rhetorical; however, I
don't believe it is possible for us to fully understand why God
decided to do things his way (and not my seemingly superior
way) and why he allows so much bad stuff to go down. But I
do think God has provided us with ample information as to
why some things are the way they are and that's a big part of
what the Bible, his Word, is all about.

According to the Bible (both Old Testament and New
Testament) there is a spiritual battle being fought in this world
that is largely invisible to us. Therefore, there are a lot of things
going on that don't seem to make a lot of sense. But the one
indisputable fact that resonates all the way through the Bible,
from Genesis to Malachi, from Matthew to Revelation, is the
fact that the king of the universe is supremely interested in
having a relationship with every single one of us.

People today like to imagine God as infinitely friendly
and politically correct. He (or just as likely, She) is a warm
and fuzzy deity who loves us unconditionally, has realistic
expectations for what we are capable of doing, and invariably

lets us off the hook whenever we mess up. Kind of like a heavenly Santa Claus. He's keeping track of when we're naughty or nice but, when push comes to shove, even the rottenest kids find something under the Christmas tree. These are pleasant enough concepts but unfortunately they are nothing at all like the ones presented in the Bible. God just doesn't fall into the *Oh, God II*, *Highway to Heaven*, or *What Dreams May Come* image of the Almighty.

Because in addition to being the embodiment of love, God is also entirely righteous and holy. We are not comfortable with this part nowadays because we have a lot of ideas about situational ethics and culturally correct conduct that make the whole idea of right and wrong seem rather archaic. But if we are prepared to understand and accept the proposition that people were created in God's image, and not the other way around, we can't keep believing God is whatever we would like him to be and not who and what he claims he is.

God, doing things his way and not my way, created people with free will. He placed the world, in pristine condition, at man's disposal and left a few instructions. Left to their own devices, our ancestors rolled their eyes at the ground rules, slipped slyly away from God's directives, and went about doing things their own way. The Bible classifies this disobedience as sin.

Sin is one of those words we don't use much these days. It sounds unenlightened and obsolete. In fact, it sounds downright backwards. After all, when people do something wrong, isn't there practically always a reason that renders their behavior excusable? Perhaps they were once abused. Perhaps they are members of a minority group. Were they intoxicated? Under-medicated? Maybe they were recently passed over for a promotion or even fired. Or maybe they just had a really, really bad day. In our society we have devised any number of rationalizations that allow people to evade responsibility for their behavior.

Even among those who believe that sin exists, there remain misconceptions. Some people think sin refers only to major violations, such as drive-by shooting, cheating on one's spouse and serial murder. Those with more sensitive consciences might throw in other behavioral infractions, like perusing a classmate's paper while taking a test or spending a little too much time with a bottle of Jack Daniels. But as God sees deep into the human heart, qualifying for sin is not an anomaly, it's an inevitability.

Because sin is not defined exclusively by behavior; it is a disposition. Nevertheless, we are accountable for every unkind thought, every selfish motive, every spurned opportunity to do the right thing. Maybe it's something as obvious as belittling your boss behind his back, faking a stomach ache to get out of doing something, or stepping on the accelerator to prevent someone from cutting in front of you in traffic. Or it may be something as subtle as avoiding a friend in need of help, leaving a mess for someone else to clean up, or drooling with envy over how easy the other guy has it. But the bottom line is that we all sin. We can't help it.

So, we're all sinners. Big deal, right? Well, actually, yes. Because God is holy, our sin creates a chasm that separates us from him and prevents us from being in right relationship with him.

But here's the good news: God loves us, even in our imperfect sinful state, and wants to establish and maintain a connection with us. And so, right from the beginning, God devised a mechanism for people to acknowledge their wrongdoing, demonstrate their contrition, and make things right with him. Initially this was an elaborate system of animal sacrifices, a central element being the annual, ritual sacrifice of a lamb (one "without spot or blemish") to atone for the sins of the entire Jewish nation for a year. Think what you will, but this is the method God established for his chosen people to obtain forgiveness and maintain a relationship with him.

And it is the same route that allows us to be with him in eternity. That's why Jesus had to die. He lived a life characterized by love, righteousness and holiness. His death is the sacrifice that "washes away" our sins and makes us acceptable to God. All we have to do is accept and receive.

By acknowledging our sin and receiving this sacrifice on our own behalf, we are crossing a bridge over the chasm that separated us from God. And once we accept the Messiah-ship of Jesus, we begin the process of allowing God to indwell us and direct our lives. Some people call this being saved or born again. It can happen to someone irrespective of whether they are Catholic or Protestant or from any other religious background. Jewish people who make this decision may be referred to as Completed Jews, Hebrew Christians, or Messianic Jews. Whatever you call it, this is the spiritual transaction that provides us with permanent peace and relationship with God.

Over the centuries there have been those who have not grasped the significance of Jesus' death and who have focused their attention on the secondary issues around his betrayal and crucifixion, some going so far as to hold the entire Jewish race responsible for his death. These people are completely missing the point.

Jesus didn't die by mistake. A Roman emperor, a religious tribunal, and a turncoat friend didn't come along unexpectedly and mess things up for the Messiah. When Jesus was dying on the cross, God wasn't in heaven shaking his head saying, "I can't believe this is happening."

Jesus came to die. Specifically. Intentionally. That's what his life was all about. So instead of people continuing to waste precious time wondering how this could have happened and trying to place blame, they would be well advised to ask why it happened.

Here are just some of the reasons. To demonstrate God's love for us. To enable an intimate relationship to form between us and God. To free us from the fear of death. To bring eternal life to all who believe in him. To unleash the power of God in our lives.

So if this is the way it is, and if there is so much scriptural evidence supporting the Messiah-ship of Jesus, why is it that relatively few Jewish people believe? Back in Jesus' day, people wondered the same thing. The apostle Paul, who I mentioned earlier, wrote about a spiritual barrier preventing Jewish people from understanding the Bible, comparing it to a veil. Paul, who had previously persecuted Jewish people who believed Jesus to be the Messiah, wrote:

"Their minds were made dull, for to this day the same veil remains when the old covenant is read. It has not been removed, because only in Christ is it taken away. Even to this day when Moses is read, a veil covers their hearts. But whenever anyone turns to the Lord, the veil is taken away" (2 Corinthians 3:14-16).

Deuteronomy 29:4 makes a similar point: "But to this day the Lord has not given you a mind that understands or eyes that see or ears that hear."

The prophet Isaiah wrote, "Go and tell this people: 'Be ever hearing, but never understanding; be ever seeing, but never perceiving'" (Isaiah 6:9).

So there it is. Until the veil is removed, the Jewish Bible is just another book. All you've got are a bunch of words that no more reveal God than a picture covered with blue and green and gray dots.

And all it takes to remove the veil is to turn to God and ask.

Chapter 11:
Slippery Times

Bill and I started a family but we were never quite able to put down roots. Two sons later we found ourselves on a journey, both educationally and vocationally driven, that led us to Athens, Georgia, various communities in the greater Dallas area, and eventually back to Massachusetts. Our peripatetic pathway lasted about fifteen years. Initially, this was an exciting and fulfilling time during which we endeavored to make God the central figure in our lives. Whenever we moved, we would locate a church that reflected our beliefs and establish connections there. While no marriage is perfect, I considered ours to be sound; we loved and respected one another and we enjoyed the challenges and rewards of parenthood. It wasn't until we returned to Massachusetts in 1985 that things began to unravel.

It is not my intention to provide a postmortem on my marriage or present a comprehensive analysis of what went wrong. In any case, back then I saw things quite differently than I do today. We were no longer compatible, we married too young, we had grown in different directions. Those are the things I remember telling myself as I began feeling increasingly trapped and unhappy in my marriage. But over the past twenty years, I have come to see things through a very different lens. A spiritual one.

What happened was that I drifted away from my relationship with God and went back to doing things on my own. The breakup of my marriage was just one element of the resulting fallout. It wasn't as if one day I made up my mind to walk away from God and sever my connections with other believers. But one thing led to another and the next thing I knew I was free-falling down a dark and slippery slope.

It started with my attitude. I had developed a penchant, practically an addiction, for zeroing in on what was wrong with other people and especially with other Christians. I considered this ability my "gift of discernment." It was amazing how astute I was in detecting the imperfections and shortcomings in virtually everyone except myself. This one was self-centered and rude. That one was a gossip and a backstabber. There were any number of hypocrites and phonies out there. And you would not believe how many critical and judgmental people I came across.

Instead of looking upward or inward, I found myself looking mostly sideways. And so, when someone would get on my nerves or hurt me or anger me, I was more than happy to write them off. This was especially true of Christian friends, because I would hold them to a higher standard than the "unsaved."

It was the same way with church. I would be irked or annoyed by the behavior of someone sitting across the aisle. I would be offended by something the pastor said in a sermon. The music wasn't to my liking or the pews weren't comfortable or the temperature in the sanctuary was too hot or too cold. It was always something and then it was always time to move on.

Church after church, disappointment after disappointment, there was not a single place where I felt I belonged, where I felt comfortable, where I felt my very reasonable criteria were all satisfactorily met. I remember the point when I told Bill that "going to church is getting in the way of my relationship with God." And that was that.

I stopped going to church. I stopped hanging out (or what we called fellowshipping) with other believers. My Bible migrated from the nightstand in my bedroom to the bookshelf in my living room to a box in my basement. My prayers devolved from multifaceted communion with God to an occasional plea for him to "gimme" this or that.

As my relationship with God became increasingly irrelevant, the whole Christian thing became downright inconvenient. While I never stopped believing in God and never stopped trusting in Jesus for my salvation, trying to live according to the Bible just mattered less and less. And then the time came when it didn't matter at all. This phenomenon is what is known in Christian circles as backsliding.

My life went from richness to ruin in very short order and, the funny thing is, I never even made the connection. I divorced. I lost my house. My sons were relegated to shuffling back and forth across town between Bill and myself. One day I was walking the walk and then, a couple of detours and side steps later, everything was a shambles.

I was now a divorcee. This was something I had never imagined back in the years I had attached bridal gowns to an endless procession of paper dolls and installed Barbie and Ken in their Dream House. As the first person in the history of my family to get a divorce, nobody had to tell me that I was a colossal failure. Granted, there was a part of me that was relieved to be a free agent and determined to make the best of things. But for the most part I was brokenhearted, guilt-ridden, and grieving.

During my marriage I had studied to become a sign language interpreter but after working in this field for a number of years I knew it just wasn't my thing. To be a good interpreter you need to be completely impartial and refrain from interjecting your own views into the communication process. Being somewhat (alright, maybe somewhat more than somewhat) outspoken and opinionated, this was a difficult task for me. As much as I enjoyed working with Deaf people and as fascinated as I remained with the beauty and complexity of American Sign Language, I realized I would probably end up with an ulcer if I didn't find some other way to make a living.

Following my divorce I went back to college. Majoring in psychology started out as the path of least resistance but by the time I graduated with a Bachelor of Science in Psychology I was genuinely interested in my studies. While I had the momentum I decided I might as well keep going and two years later I had a Masters in Social Work. Completing my education provided me with a sense of accomplishment and opened the door to my career as a clinical social worker. Timing is everything. The psychiatric hospital where I had been working as a sign language interpreter had a social work opening just as I was finishing graduate school.

I bit the bullet on spending and eventually saved up enough to purchase my own home. Sometimes I felt like Sally Fields in one of those movies where she fights all odds to save the farm or organize the union or accomplish some other spunky feat. But more and more often I was sad and defeated, going through the motions of living, trying to make sense of my life.

From all outward appearances, I was moving forward and moving on, making something of myself. But on the inside, it was something else entirely. During the years I wandered in this spiritual wasteland, I was empty and aching, looking for something or someone to take away the pain. I stopped playing by the biblical rules and made up some of my own. Self-determination took the place of the Thou Shalt Not's. Situational ethics took the place of the Beatitudes. The more time passed, the less sensitive my conscience became, and the easier it was to find ways to justify or rationalize whatever I wanted to do.

I sank deeper into my self-imposed misery. My dysthymia, that low-level, lingering depression, returned with a vengeance. While it wasn't a major clinical depression, it was still enough to suck most of the joy right out of my life. You probably wouldn't have noticed. I inherited the actress gene from my mother and was capable of putting on a pretty decent performance when I put my mind to it. I also got her privacy gene and didn't let many people in close enough to notice my pain.

This is the way things were for me for about eighteen years. Everything was okay on the outside and downright miserable on the inside. But somehow I endured.

And then one day in June 2004, out of the blue, I received an email from a friend I hadn't seen in years inviting me to a Bible Study in her home. A Bible Study? A Bible Study! Fat chance. But for some reason I couldn't get that invitation out of my mind. And then I thought, why not? I figured there was nothing that could make me feel any worse than I was already feeling, so what did I have to lose?

And that was how my life got turned back around. About a week or so later I was sitting in my friend Val's living room when something mysterious and wonderful occurred. As Val began teaching the lesson she had prepared, it was as if every word coming out of her mouth was directed straight at me so that, rather than listening to her, I was listening to God.

I sat there, immobile, barely able to breathe, with that paralyzed feeling you get sometimes in a dream. And as

Val spoke -- I cannot remember a word of what she said -- I felt God's love and forgiveness pulling me powerfully and permanently out of the darkness and back into the light. That night I went home, made my peace with God, and recommitted myself to turning my life around and trying to make it count for something.

You know how it is when you've been sick with a bad case of the flu? It's like nothing else really matters, and every day your whole world just keeps getting smaller and smaller until it's all about you. "I'm hot!" "I'm cold!" "I need my pill!" "Will you get me some juice?" It gets to the point where the whole universe seems to revolve around you being sick and you just cannot imagine a day when you will ever feel any differently.

And then, after what seems like a lifetime of coughing and after you've produced enough used Kleenex to fill a swimming pool and after everyone in your family has learned to tip-toe past your room lest you pester them to fluff your pillow for the fifty-seventh time, it's over. Suddenly comes the day when you're not sick any more. You know: the first day you don't need a nap and when you can figure out for yourself that it's high time you took a shower?

There's a Pink Floyd song called "Coming Back to Life" and that's what it felt like after I got off my spiritual sickbed and recommitted my life to God. It's impossible to describe the sense of relief, renewal, and recovery I have felt since getting back on track. All I can say is that even the most uneventful day spent in relationship with God beats the best possible day living under the sick spell of the world. Grateful doesn't even begin to describe it. It just feels so good not to feel bad.

Since that day in June 2004, I've been able to come to grips with some of the mistakes I made and move forward. Fortunately, I happen to have a God who specializes in the impossible. Bringing life from death? Not a problem. Looks like a pile of dust? Nope, it's the makings of a man. Failure and defeat are material for transformation and victory in the hands of my God and so rehabilitating a backslider like me is right up his alley.

Although I think of those dark years with sadness, I do not operate under a burden of shame and guilt. Forgiven means forgiven. My sins are in the bottom of the ocean (Micah 7:19). "As far as east is from the west, so far has he removed our transgressions from us" (Psalm 103:12).

God has revealed himself to me more powerfully and more compassionately in the past few years than I could possibly describe. As my friend Val said to me once, "You left him but he never left you."

Chapter 12:
Back on Track

I know a gifted guitarist who is also something of an intellectual. While I'm relaxing my brain watching *Project Runway* or *Top Chef*, he's tuned in to the History or Discovery channel, always in the process of learning something new. But my guitar-playing friend says that no matter how much he learns about any given subject (the civil war, astronomy, Greek philosophy, physics), there will never be anything as remotely interesting or satisfying as the world of music. Every aspect, from composition to technique to style to performance, brings with it a multitude of complexity and challenge that will keep him forever intrigued. And even though complete mastery of any given element is inherently and ultimately out of reach, the very pursuit of excellence is of sufficient pleasure and value as to make every other field of inquiry pale in comparison.

That's exactly how I would characterize my relationship with God. The levels of understanding and the challenges of living according to his directives are countless. Think about it. God -- the Supreme Being, the Alpha and Omega, the Creator of the Universe -- wants to be intimately involved in every aspect of our lives. Our thoughts, our emotions, our relationships, all of our day-to-day comings and goings; that covers a lot of territory. In fact, it's endless. But God doesn't crash the party; his participation in our personal lives is by invitation only.

My decision to accept God's terms for relationship with him was only the beginning. Having acknowledged my sinful nature and been reconciled to God by the Messiah's sacrifice, the real adventure began.

Sometimes I think of it as living in a parallel universe. Outwardly I am doing the same things everyone else is doing. Getting up in the morning, going to work, socializing, shopping. Cooking dinner, paying my bills, emptying the dishwasher, taking out the trash. But inwardly there is a whole other level of being: the challenge and struggle and blessing and reward of learning to live in a way that is consistent with the Bible. I might as well tell you, it ain't easy. I'm not even close to being the kind of person I am striving to become. But there is nothing, nothing at all, nothing whatsoever, that can even compare with the pure joy of trying.

Preachers are fond of saying that God has a plan for every person's life. Some even insist that it is his ultimate plan to fix all our problems and make us rich. And while there are certainly instances where things have gone exceedingly well for various individuals and people have accumulated massive amounts of wealth, God is a whole lot more interested in what might be characterized as an inner prosperity.

His plan is to get us into shape, spiritually speaking, so we can be of some use to him in this world and are better suited for the world to come. God takes pleasure in working through us and so the more in tune with him we are, the more use we can be to those around us. It is gratifying and humbling to realize how much potential there is for even one person to impact the world.

Because no matter how good we have it during our brief stay on this planet, the only thing we take with us is our character, our inner selves. The BMWs, swimming pools, iPods, and plasma TV's stay. The six-pack abs, bleached teeth, and designer duds all turn to dust. While most of us can't help being impressed by these things, God isn't. What matters most to him are those things that are eternal…like our souls.

I don't want to leave you with the impression that the Christian life is one of deprivation and drudgery, because nothing could be further from the truth. Knowing the living God and living in relationship with him is satisfying and rewarding in a way that nothing else can possibly be, because this is the purpose for which we were created. At times it can be almost unbearably exciting. At other times it can be excruciatingly difficult. Day by day, and sometimes even moment by moment, it is practically always challenging.

Socrates taught that the unexamined life is not worth living. Christianity takes that a step further by suggesting it should be God doing the examining and not we ourselves.

Under the lens of the Bible, God's Word, we have an instruction manual that gives us all the direction we will ever need with respect to how we should be living. Under the leading of God's Spirit we get additional guidance and "course corrections" as we go about our lives. With connections to other believers, we get the love, support, and encouragement we need to continue along this path, even when the going gets tough.

How has all of this been working out for me? It is definitely a process. And since my June 2004 experience, I don't take one single thing about my relationship with God for granted.

Every day I make it a priority to spend time in prayer and reading the Bible. I acknowledge the areas where I have been at fault and receive God's forgiveness. I assume an attitude of forgiveness toward individuals who have hurt or offended me in some way. I pray for others. I ask God for wisdom and direction in specific areas. I meditate on how I might apply some truth, some principle of scripture to my life. I make a conscious decision to obey God. I succeed. I fail. I struggle. I grow.

As I am seeking to yield to God in some matter it feels like climbing a mountain. But when I finally achieve a measure of success in that particular area I find myself, not on a mountain top, but at a higher elevation from which I am able to see another incline, another distant peak, another something that God has placed in my path to challenge and refine me. The further along I go, the higher the elevation, and the more I realize how much is still before me. But far from discouraging, this is a process that is exhilarating and exciting. Difficult? Sure. But never boring.

The thing it most often comes down to is love. Loving God means loving people, not in some theoretical abstract manner but in practical, tangible terms. Treating people with kindness and respect and looking out for the needs of others is a whole lot easier said than done, as I discovered back in Watts in 1970. It is a personal relationship with God that provides the power to genuinely put the interests of others above our own.

Probably the biggest testing ground for me is at work. For many years, I have been a clinical social worker on a locked inpatient unit, working with adults who are diagnosed with major mental illnesses like schizophrenia, bipolar disorder, post-traumatic stress disorder, and major depression. In order to be eligible to receive this level of care people have to meet commitment criteria, meaning their mental illnesses have rendered them a danger to themselves, a danger to others, or unable to care for themselves safely in the community.

This is interesting work, as you can probably imagine. But while it can be rewarding at times, it also has the potential to be quite stressful and discouraging. There are few places where it is more difficult for me to put my faith into action.

Let's take just one verse, Philippians 2:14: "Do everything without complaining or arguing." This is not just a matter of human effort. In fact, human effort in this kind of pursuit only leaves me feeling exhausted and defeated. Even if I manage to refrain from verbal complaint or argument, I may still be harboring these attitudes in my heart. The secret to success is in focusing my attention on my relationship with God and asking for him to indwell me and to guide and direct me throughout the day. When I do that, everything else is effortless, and I find myself being the kind of person I want to be without my knuckles turning white.

It's simple enough in theory, but not always easy. Especially at work, due in part to all of the distractions and disturbances that I face on a daily basis. There are patients who are tormented by "voices" or intrusive thoughts and who feel compelled to do things that are dangerous and destructive. Patients who live in a state of constant outrage because they believe they are being "illegally incarcerated." Patients who have lived though unspeakable trauma that has left them vulnerable and despairing. Patients who want nothing more than to spend time talking with me, but for whom no amount of time is ever enough. Patients who insult, denigrate, or even assault me and my co-workers. Patients who are in unremitting psychic distress because they believe they are responsible for every terrible event they see on the evening news. Patients who make unreasonable demands at unreasonable times and file complaints when their needs are not immediately met. Patients whose anguish is so enormous they are unable to consider any solution apart from suicide.

These patients also happen to be human beings, most of whom will compliment me when I'm wearing a new outfit. Most of whom will say "have a nice weekend" when they see me exiting the unit on Friday afternoon, leaving them to their "heart-healthy" diets, four daily smoke breaks, and communal television set.

And then there are the families. Devastated parents whose children refuse to speak with them because they believe they are imposters or agents of the CIA. Brokenhearted children who are hoping for a new medication or treatment strategy that will help their desperately tormented mothers or fathers. Stalwart husbands and wives, sisters and brothers, and close family friends who have stuck by their loved ones over years of multiple hospitalizations, failed medication trials, and unsuccessful residential placements.

These are the people who invariably thank me for what I do to help their family members, even when the progress is slow, even when the outcome is tragic.

I have the pleasure of working with some wonderfully gifted colleagues on a multi-disciplinary treatment team. Social workers, psychiatrists, nurses, mental health aides, and many others collaborate in helping patients get the treatment they need to mitigate the symptoms of their mental illnesses and improve the quality of their lives. Despite the difficulties and frustrations of working with this population, we all manage to get along pretty well and we even have some fun in the process. But not always. Inpatient psychiatric work brings out the best in people...and the worst. Trying to maintain Christian principles in this setting is what I think of as graduate level Christianity.

Most of the time, I consider this work a calling of which I am undeserving. And so I give it all I've got. Due to various constraints, I do not have the freedom to speak freely with my patients or their families about matters of faith. However, it is my privilege to be able to provide treatment to these patients and their families and to pray for them. And as far as I know there is still no law against prayer.

It's still not necessarily easy being me. For one thing, I tend to be pretty hard on myself. And like I've already said, I'm not exactly the happy-go-lucky type. I relate quite a bit to Woody Allen. A few years ago when Katie Couric interviewed him on *The Today Show*, she opined he was probably the kind of person who saw the glass as half empty versus half full. Woody Allen replied, "You mean there's a glass?"

We are all born with certain dispositions and mine is inclined toward the melancholy. I'm probably never going to be the kind of person who can "take it easy" and "go with the flow." Although I've developed a tendency to camouflage this trait with the cracking of jokes, beneath the surface I am someone who takes life quite seriously. My primary point of sadness is based on the concern that there are people I love who may go through life -- and face death -- without having met the Messiah.

But here's the thing. I'm not depressed any more. Having turned back to God hasn't solved all my problems or plugged up all the holes in my life. But it has allowed me to find a measure of peace and joy that far transcends my circumstances.

Christians are dealt the same cards as everyone else: major illnesses, strained finances, family problems, unemployment. But the thing that sets us apart is the comfort that comes with being able to share our trials and burdens directly with God. There is enormous consolation in knowing that "In all things God works for the good of those who love him, who have been called according to his purpose" (Romans 8:28).

To the extent that I invite God to participate in my life, he does. Whether it involves my relationships, my work, my finances, my diet, my travel, or my investments, there is absolutely nothing that is not of interest to God, no area where he does not have relevance. Common sense and personal preference are not in any way contrary to living a Christian life. But the more I let him in, the more I realize the levels of surrender that are possible, if I am so inclined.

I walked away from all of this once. I paid the price in emptiness and sadness and there were others who suffered the consequences of my decision as well. But God is a God of forgiveness and second chances and new beginnings. So now I've got another shot at it. Without the arrogance of youth, without the naiveté of inexperience, I'm seeing things a lot differently than I did back when I was twenty. And while I have a tendency to laugh at practically everything else, I am seriously serious when it comes to God.

What it all boils down to is this: I can't afford to make another big mistake. There once was a time when it was alright for me to crawl and toddle and tumble and fall, but those days are over. I just don't have the luxury of making another eighteen-year blunder. So to the best of my ability, with God's help, with the support of my Christian friends, I plan to get it right this time. By this I mean I'm keeping my eye on him and not letting anything else get in the way. No more stamping my feet, throwing a fit, and walking away when the going gets tough. No more hemming and hawing when God gives me a little something to do. No more picking and choosing which scriptures to apply to my life and rationalizing away the ones which are inconvenient. No more halfhearted, "well, that was true back in Jesus' day but it doesn't necessarily apply today" thinking.

I guess I'm not such a big wise-guy any more. I know that I'm not beyond being tempted and deceived again. These days I try to keep short accounts with God. Acknowledging sin, confessing my failings, and accepting his forgiveness is not something reserved for Yom Kippur. Obedience to the Bible is not something reserved for rabbis, priests and pastors.

Don't think my determination is fanaticism born out of remorse or an attempt to earn brownie points with God. What's happening here is nothing more and nothing less than gratitude to God for bringing me out from darkness into the light, not once but twice. And it's because I know, first hand, that there is absolutely no satisfaction, no peace, no real joy in anything other than walking in fellowship with God.

Chapter 13:
High Stakes

Remember back when I was talking about how I would have done things if I were God? I was basing my beneficence on maximizing creature comforts and building upon the passing pleasures of this temporal world. God's way takes into account so much more. It embraces a spiritual realm that we can barely comprehend. And it includes the capacity for eternal life, which will render things like fancy jewelry and fast cars meaningless. There is a depth to God's love which is so profound that once we grab hold of even the slightest bit of it there is no letting go.

But just as powerful as God's love is his holiness. He designed the world based on certain principles, including the one that requires the shedding of blood in order to allow the forgiveness of sin. I know, I know, that's not the way I would have done it either. "My thoughts are not your thoughts, neither are your ways my ways, declares the Lord" (Isaiah 55:8).

So unless you think you have met God's standard of perfection and have lived an exemplary life, a life completely free of deceit, envy, judgment, selfishness, insensitivity, and pride, there is a chasm separating you from God. And because a holy God requires justice, the only way to bridge this gap is to accept the sacrifice of the Messiah.

When Jesus said, "I am the way and the truth and the life. No one comes to the Father except through me" (John 14:6), this is what he was talking about. And this is pretty much where the rubber hits the road with respect to how Christianity differs from any other religion or belief system. Moses never made these claims. Neither did Buddha or Confucius or Mohammed or any of the Dalai Lamas.

In making this statement, Jesus was either unspeakably arrogant, appallingly deluded, a con merchant of the first degree, or he was who he said he was. There is really no middle ground here and people who try to characterize Jesus as a great teacher or role model haven't done their homework. Great men don't go around claiming to be the Messiah. Except for Jesus.

Religions instructing you to be good and not to be bad are a dime a dozen. Religions offering ritual and tradition can be found on every street corner. Practically every religion comes complete with literature and liturgy. But there is only one faith that is entirely based upon the sacrifice of a savior.

We are living in a very narcissistic time. "It's all about me," we joke, but fundamentally believe. "I deserve to be happy," we proclaim unabashedly to others or think silently to ourselves. We are encouraged, no, practically commanded, to take excellent care of ourselves and to spare no expense in doing so. And there is no guilt, no shame, no dishonor in openly putting our own needs before the needs of anybody else.

Then there is the seductive lure of materialism. With the onslaught of advertising from every element of the media and with the plethora of purchasing options available through malls, catalogues, and the internet, there is an unprecedented level of consumerism in our world today. We spend unconscionable amounts of time and money on our clothes, our cars, our homes, our vacations. It is practically impossible not to get caught up in it. Sure, we extend ourselves and our resources to our families and friends, but this is still a people-based generosity. Even those of us who are environmentally progressive or have social consciences think it's all about mankind or our planet, wanting to leave the world a better place for our children and grandchildren.

I am all for protecting our environment. And I do not believe there is anything inherently wrong with having nice things. I like nice things. God does too. Just look around and you will get a sense of the depth and breadth and volume of beauty that has been provided for us, courtesy of our creator. There is nothing in nature that is not inherently capable of inspiring awe.

Or read the Book of Exodus, beginning in Chapter 25, and see how particular God was regarding the design and construction of items to be used within his temple. There are specific instructions regarding tables, chairs, lamp-stands, curtains, and screens. There are even detailed directions regarding the garments to be worn by the priests. When you read about all the gold and silver and precious gems involved, you will see that God has nothing whatsoever against the finer things in life. Why would he? He created them.

The problem arises when we lose sight of the fact that the purpose of possessions is to bring us into a place of greater gratitude and appreciation for our creator. But all too often, our preoccupation with the trappings of the physical world is the very thing that prevents us from attending to the spiritual one.

Perhaps the greatest shared delusion we have is that God is whatever we envision Him/Her/It to be. Our post-modern society declares, "There are many paths to God." There are any number of books and movies promoting the idea that heaven will turn out to be however you imagine it in your mind, whether it be eternal life in an amusement park or diving into an endless succession of Impressionist period watercolors. The very idea of God being defined in one particular manner is considered immature and narrow-minded. And so there has emerged a default theology in which every individual gets to define God for himself.

What it all boils down to is that we attempt to create God in our image. If we believe in him at all, that is.

But it's not all about us. It's not about our comfort, our pleasure, and our personal satisfaction. It's not about our friends and families, our towns and states, our nations and our planet. It's not even about our solar system or the galaxies beyond. It's all about him.

God made the world for his purposes and for his pleasure. It doesn't matter whether or not we believe it. It doesn't matter if we have a different perspective or mindset. It doesn't even matter if we are "uncomfortable" with the idea that God sets all the terms regarding holiness and sin and the need for forgiveness. Whether or not we object to the very idea of spiritual absolutes, this is the way it is.

God woos us. He reveals himself to us through the beauty and majesty of nature. We see his power in the grandeur of the universe. We see his love in the gift of a child. It takes an incredible amount of denial or arrogance or narcissism to believe that all of creation is without a creator. However, the world in which we live is not engineered to bring us a plethora of passing pleasures or temporal good times. It is designed to bring us to him.

He calls us. Again, there are any number of ways. It may be through the circumstances of your life, a trial so impossible that you have nowhere to look but upward or a burden so heavy you cannot bear it alone. It may be an intellectual pursuit or a spiritual journey. It may be a terminal diagnosis or a fiery moment in a foxhole or the ring of your telephone at three o'clock in the morning that gets your attention. But whatever it is, there may come a time in your life when the answers you currently have just aren't enough.

God is broadcasting 24-7, but some people don't seem especially interested in hearing the program. Many won't even tune in to the frequency. There are any number of reasons, any number of objections. I've heard quite a few over the years.

My friend Jaclyn says, "I'm happy with my life. I don't need God to help me lead a better life or be a better person."

To Jaclyn I say: I'm glad you are happy and that you feel good about yourself and about the way you conduct your life. But Christianity is not a matter of how you feel or what you do. It's a matter of understanding that God has an agenda that supercedes our own.

My friend Gregory says, "What about those people living in distant places where missionaries have never gone? If Jesus is the only way to salvation, what about them?"

To Gregory I say: I don't presume to know how God reaches those who have never heard the message about Jesus. I believe this is among the many mysteries we will someday understand. And your question is only the tip of the iceberg. What about the developmentally disabled and cognitively impaired? What about infants and children who die before they are capable of making this kind of decision? While I don't understand why these tragedies occur, I do know that God is fair, loving, and just, and that ignorance in these matters is not an excuse for refusing the gift of salvation that God is holding out to each one of us.

My mother says, "I don't believe the part about the fish. How could two pieces of fish be enough to feed five thousand people? It's just not possible."

To my mom I say: I am impressed. To think that you took the time and made the effort to begin reading the New

Testament! And I am further impressed that you made it all the way through the virgin birth, the calming of the waves, the casting out of evil spirits, and the healing of blind men and lepers, before you got derailed by the miracle of the loaves and the fish.

The way I see it, if you can believe in a God who created the laws of nature and physics, how can you not believe he has the power to reconfigure atoms (or whatever it takes) to override his own rules? My suggestion to you would be to not get hung up on things you can't understand, but to put them on "hold." It's like watching a movie. You might miss some things in the beginning -- a line of dialogue, a minor plot twist -- but by the end everything comes together and it all makes sense.

My friend Mackenzie says, "Jesus was just a Jewish guy people made into a martyr."

To Mackenzie I first say: You are right on one count. Jesus was a Jewish guy, at least on his mother's side. But it would not be accurate to classify him as a martyr, someone who chooses to die rather than renouncing religious principles. Jesus didn't die for a cause...he died for us. His death was a spiritual transaction to make peace between us and God.

All of the above are understandable and legitimate concerns; undoubtedly there are many more. And while I don't think coming to faith is simply a matter of intellectual persuasion, I do believe the facts in the Bible stand up to scrutiny and that the mysteries and unanswered questions will not dissuade anyone with a seeking heart and an open mind from believing. The bottom line is that there are no acceptable excuses for turning away from God when he is reaching out to you.

God loves us and wants us to know him, not as a vague, amorphous abstraction, but as a Father. He has a plan for every single person and is engineering the circumstances in our lives to accomplish his purposes. This includes the very fact that you are reading this book.

Perhaps you are someone who already understands, believes, and accepts what I've been saying. You recognize the fact that you are a sinner and you believe that Jesus died in your place. You have already had a conversation -- a prayer -- with God, during which you acknowledged this and accepted the gift of salvation.

The prayer I said back in 1970 went something like this:

"Dear God, I know that I am a sinner and that my sin separates me from you. Thank you for sending your son, Jesus the Messiah, to die in my place, so that my sins can be forgiven. I accept this sacrifice. I ask you to take control of my life and complete the process of helping me become the person you have created me to be. Amen."

You may have prayed a prayer like this one decades ago. Or maybe it was just within the last few minutes. There's no magic formula or specific language that you need to use, just as long as the prayer comes from your heart. If you have done this, your sins are forgiven, there is peace between you and God, and you are a full citizen in his kingdom. And the more time you spend developing your relationship with God, the more you will experience the sense of peace that comes with knowing that the creator of the universe has embraced you as his child. You also have the assurance of knowing that on the day you face God, your entry into heaven is guaranteed because of the blood the Messiah shed on your behalf.

But perhaps you are someone who is viewing my story and understanding of God with skepticism, cynicism, or outright disbelief. You may think this is all a bunch of nonsense or superstition or mistaken interpretation or worse. But are you sure?

Consider for a moment the possibility, even the remote possibility, that what I am saying is correct. That would mean that you are mistaken. And the implications about being wrong about something of this magnitude are unimaginable. These are high stakes.

Have you ever been involved in a tragedy that could have been averted had you done something differently? If you had only been wearing your seatbelt the day that truck plowed into you, you wouldn't be rolling through the rest of your life in a wheelchair. If you had only stopped smoking back when you promised yourself you would, you wouldn't weigh ninety-five pounds and be fighting a losing battle with lung cancer. If you had only listened to your brother-in-law and bought a few shares of that stock he was touting last year, you'd be spending the rest of your life wintering in the Bahamas instead of trying to make a few extra bucks plowing out driveways. If only, if only, if only; but in life, there is no going back. That sick feeling in your stomach, that deep sorrow and regret, will not change a situation that is irreversible.

And that's the way it is with this decision. You can go your own way, assume you're correct, take your chances that there is no God and no afterlife. You can cross your fingers and hope for a Santa Claus type of God whose jolly disposition will override any responsibility on your part. Or you can perform your occasional Do-Unto-Other's and trust that being better than the guy next door will place you in good enough stead in the remote chance there is a judgment day in your future.

But suppose you're wrong? That would mean God will some day hold you accountable for the totality of your behavior, the entirety of your inner life, and your very disposition. And at that point, it will be too late.

Revelation, the last book of the Bible, talks about a day of judgment and something called the Book of Life. All those who have acknowledged their sin and accepted Jesus' sacrifice on their behalf have their names inscribed in this book. This means they will not be judged on the basis of their own righteousness, or lack thereof, but based on the righteousness of the Messiah in whom they have placed their trust. This ensures God's complete forgiveness and their entry into heaven. God's heaven, not the Hollywood version.

On the other hand, people who have some other plan for how they want to represent themselves to the creator of the universe are probably not going to be too happy with the outcome. And at that point, there are no "do overs." Like they say on those so-called reality shows: you're in or you're out.

Whatever your objections, whatever your reservations, whatever your resistance to making the decision to take that step of faith, I ask you to consider again. God is waiting for you with outstretched arms. He sent his son, the Messiah, to pay the price for your sin and close the gap that separates you from him. You don't have to join a church or send a check or fill out any forms. This is a transaction on a spiritual order. All that is required is an acknowledgement of your unworthiness and a willingness to accept God's provision for your salvation.

Some of you would like to believe this but aren't quite there. You don't want to play the odds that might have you spending eternity somewhere apart from the presence of God. But at the same time, you don't want to be a hypocrite and recite a prayer that you don't really mean. To you I would say, try doing what I did back in Santa Cruz.

Talk to God. In your own words. Tell him you want to know the truth about who he is. Ask him to reveal himself to you. Then get yourself a New Testament and start reading. I suggest you begin with the book of John; it is a clear, comprehensive, and powerful account. If you will do this with an open mind and a humble heart, I have no doubt that God will meet you there.

Or go ahead and do it. Accept the sacrifice of the Messiah with whatever degree of conviction you may have. Your very willingness to meet God on his terms, your own uncertainty notwithstanding, is a powerful step of faith. God will honor your willingness to take that shaky first step. And if you will continue to seek him in the Bible, he will take you the rest of the way.

But whatever you do, do something. Ignoring God is tantamount to rejecting him. He is standing at the door of your life and knocking.

"Now is the day of salvation" (2 Corinthians 6:2).

Now is the time to let him in.

Final Words

Jews for Jesus is an excellent resource for people (both Jewish and Gentile) interested in knowing more about Biblical prophecy, the historical facts about Jesus, the manner in which Jewish people integrate belief in Jesus into their lives, and the steps to "get saved."

The *Jews for Jesus* website provides a wealth of information, including the following:

Answers:
Addresses common questions and objections about Jesus;

Personal Stories:
The experiences of various Jewish believers;

Videos:
These include stories of Jews who survived the Holocaust;

Forum:
Allows expression of views (often controversial) on various topics;

Chat Room:
Venue for further discussion;

Contact Us Link:
Where questions may be submitted confidentially;

Bookstore:
Offering books, music, DVDs, and other materials.

Website: JewsForJesus.org

Jews for Jesus may also be contacted at:

Jews for Jesus
60 Haight Street
San Francisco, CA 94102

Phone: 415-864-2600

Email: jfj@jewsforjesus.org

Acknowledgements

I want to express my appreciation to Peter & Jan Bryan, Barbara Ford, Avi & Leah Brickner, Pat Lane (a.k.a. The Grammar Nazi), and Stan Telchin. Your support, advice, constructive criticism, and prayers were essential in transforming my manuscript into a book.

Thanks also to the family and friends who inspired me to write this book and encouraged me along the way: Daniel Sogolow, Noah & Karin Sogolow, Donna Fazekas, Paul Fazekas (last one on *Oprah* is a rotten egg), Gail Janukowicz (how's my hair?), Rob Janukowicz, John & Rayna Notta, Andrea Notta (graphic artist extraordinaire), Kenneth & Robin Spencer, Jonathan & Suzi Fingerhut, Susan Bass, Sheryl Ethier, Felicia Bryan, Kim Maibaum, and Ene & Esther Ette.

And my deepest love and gratitude to Jack Pike for believing in me, sharing my vision, and having faith in the potential of my book. Without your love and support I would never have been able to bring this project to completion. We then shall live, my love.

The author may be contacted at:

messiahandme@yahoo.com

Printed in the United States
118784LV00001B/1-60/P